DAVENPORT'S
NEW JERSEY
WILLS AND
ESTATE PLANNING
LEGAL FORMS

DAVENPORT'S NEW JERSEY WILLS AND ESTATE PLANNING LEGAL FORMS

2024 EDITION

written by attorneys
Alex Russell and Robert Maxwell

**SEE BOOKS AND LEGAL FORMS AT
WWW.DAVENPORTPUBLISHING.COM**

COPYRIGHT © 2024 -- ALEX RUSSELL

CREATIVE COMMONS LICENSE. This work is also licensed under a Creative Commons Attribution-NonCommercial-NoDerivatives 4.0 International License.

GOVERNMENT WORKS. No claim is made to copyright or ownership of government materials.

SOME STANDARD FORMS. No copyright or ownership is claimed of "standard" forms or leading forms for the state which are provided in this book, but fair use and privilege to use is claimed. Makers of such forms (often a state agency or hospital) have agreed by word, act, and implication the forms may be used and copied if no profit is sought and no substantial changes made to them. Such makers if not a lawyer or law firm are barred from profit or advantage in practicing law by making forms then limiting use. Forms and other related materials are used here for educational purposes only. Authors strongly believe in a religious duty to help people and do charity.

PUBLICATION DATA
(informal, library may use different data)

Names: Russell, Alex, 1972- author; Maxwell, Robert, 1960- author

Title: Davenport's New Jersey Wills And Estate Planning Legal Forms 2024 Edition

Other Titles: Davenport's Wills

Description: Davenport Publishing 2024

Suggested Identifiers: LCCN 2021909030
9798355688004
9798748423373
ISBN 9798748423373

Subjects: LCSH: Wills--United States;
Wills--United States--Forms;
Estate Planning--United States;
Legal Forms

Classification: LFF KF755 .C55 2024 (or as library chooses)
DDC 346.73 Rus--dc24 (or as library chooses)

9 8 7 6 5 4 3 2 1 0 0 0 0 0 2 4

PERMISSION TO COPY AND USE BOOKS FOR FREE

To help people and groups publisher and authors of the book allow mostly free use by giving all a "Creative Commons Attribution-NonCommercial-NoDerivatives 4.0 International License".

Basically as image below shows copying or use is OK if it still shows it's **by** the named authors, is **non-commercial** with no price charged, and has **no derivatives** which means no big changes.

Most users face no limit on copying, using, holding in library to loan out, or giving out copies.

Permission is given to change margins and formatting, do small changes, and cut any blank pages that may occur (but double-check page numbers and table of contents page numbers).

Printing on only 1 side of pages avoids complication of writing on back. Text margins are .75 inches. To do a book not a pamphlet increase left (inside) and decrease right (outside) margins.

Users can design a cover they like but the book title and author names must still appear on it.

Email questions to **davenportpress@gmail.com**.

(This work licensed under a Creative Commons Attribution-NonCommercial-NoDerivatives 4.0 International License.)

FOR FREE COPIES USE WWW.DAVENPORTPUBLISHING.COM OR BUY AT AMAZON.COM.

WARNING

THIS PUBLICATION IS NOT A SUBSTITUTE FOR LEGAL ADVICE. Publisher and authors say and warn this publication is not giving any legal, accounting, or other professional services or advice, which if wanted can be obtained by consulting in person an attorney or some other professional. **No attorney-client relationship or any relationship creating a duty or obligation is agreed to or created by the purchase or use of this publication or forms.**

BOOKS AND FORMS FOR OTHER STATES ARE AVAILABLE, SEE WWW.DAVENPORTPUBLISHING.COM FOR INFORMATION

CHAPTER	TABLE OF CONTENTS	PAGE NUMBER
CHAPTER 1 – BOOK BASICS AND LIST OF FORMS		1
CHAPTER 2 – TERMS, PROPERTY LAW, AND HELPFUL INFORMATION FORM		4
CHAPTER 3 – WILL BASICS		8
CHAPTER 4 – WILL GIFTS INCLUDING RESIDUE		10
CHAPTER 5 – DEBT, MARRIAGE, AND YOUNG CHILD ISSUES		15
CHAPTER 6 – BASIC IDEAS ABOUT HEALTH CARE FORMS		18

WILL RELATED FORMS

CHAPTER 7 – FORM 1: WILL (STANDARD)		19
CHAPTER 8 – FORM 2: WILL (GUARDIAN)		23
CHAPTER 9 – FORM 3: SELF-PROVING AFFIDAVIT		27
CHAPTER 10 – FORM 4: TANGIBLE PERSONAL PROPERTY MEMORANDUM		29
CHAPTER 11 – FORM 5: HANDWRITTEN WILL		31

HEALTH CARE FORMS

CHAPTER 12 – FORM 6: PROXY DIRECTIVE		33
CHAPTER 13 – FORM 7: INSTRUCTION DIRECTIVE		36
CHAPTER 14 – FORM 8: PRACTITIONER ORDERS FOR LIFE-SUSTAINING TREATMENT		42

GIVING POWER FORMS

CHAPTER 15 – FORM 9: DURABLE GENERAL POWER OF ATTORNEY		45
CHAPTER 16 – FORM 10: POWER OF ATTORNEY AND DELEGATION OF AUTHORITY BY PARENT CONCERNING MINOR CHILD		48
CHAPTER 17 – FORM 11: APPOINTMENT OF AGENT TO CONTROL THE FUNERAL AND DISPOSITION OF REMAINS		53

APPENDIX – SAMPLE FILLED OUT LEGAL FORMS		57

CHAPTER 1
BOOK BASICS AND LIST OF FORMS

ESTATE PLANNING CONTROLS THINGS IF LATER ABSENT, SICK, OR DEAD

This book helps people in New Jersey do legal documents to control their health care, property, money, children, funeral, and more if later they are absent, sick, or dead. Doing this is called "Estate Planning".

ESTATE PLANNING MOSTLY IS DOING SIMPLE THINGS IN 3 AREAS

Estate Planning is mostly doing simple things in 3 areas: <u>Will Related</u>, <u>Health Care</u>, and <u>Giving Power</u>. This book has 11 ready to use New Jersey legal forms (but most people use <u>just a few</u> of these forms).

WILL RELATED FORMS

<u>**Form 1. Will (Standard)**</u> – a Will (also called a "Last Will And Testament") lets a person control things after their death like who gets money and property, who is Executor, and if easier legal options can be used.

<u>**Form 2. Will (Guardian)**</u> – Will with part added to name a person to be Guardian to care for a minor child under 18 if needed (like if both parents later die) and also manage a child's property and money.

<u>**Form 3. Self-Proving Affidavit**</u> – optional form done with a Will to later help use a Will after a death.

<u>**Form 4. Tangible Personal Property Memorandum**</u> – lets a person easily write out more gifts to occur after death, but this can only cover "tangible personal property" like furniture, cars, jewelry, and clothes.

<u>**Form 5. Handwritten Will**</u> – this Will can be completed more easily by skipping the usual legally needed 2 witnesses, but by law to do this it must be all handwritten by the person doing the Will.

HEALTH CARE FORMS

<u>**Form 6. Proxy Directive**</u> – this form, also called a "Durable Power Of Attorney For Health Care", lets a person name someone to if needed later control health care and also write health care instructions.

<u>**Form 7. Instruction Directive**</u> – this form, also called a "Living Will", does the serious act of saying stop health care if <u>later</u> doctors think a person is incapacitated, in very bad health, and more care won't help.

<u>**Form 8. Practitioner Orders for Life-Sustaining Treatment**</u> – this form does the serious act of saying <u>immediately</u> no longer try most medical care including C.P.R., and this is a <u>short form</u> that can be read fast by paramedics and similar people (this is often called by people the "Do-Not-Resuscitate" form).

GIVING POWER FORMS

<u>**Form 9. Durable General Power Of Attorney**</u> – lets power over money, property, and other things be shared during person's life with a trusted person like a spouse, adult child, or friend so they can do things.

<u>**Form 10. Power Of Attorney And Delegation Of Authority By Parent Concerning Minor Child**</u> – lets parents share power over a child under 18 with a person so they have power to help care for a child.

<u>**Form 11. Appointment of Agent to Control the Funeral and Disposition of Remains**</u> – lets a person give instructions and name a person to later after their death control their funeral and related matters.

NEW JERSEY LAW ON ESTATE PLANNING COVERS MOST PEOPLE HERE

This book is only for New Jersey since Estate Planning laws and legal documents do vary between states. Usually a state's Estate Planning law applies if a person's primary residence is here (called their "domicile"). Many judges say "residence" occurs if a person lives in a place and has no clear plans to leave. Later plans to move don't matter till people move. People can stay under a previous state's Estate Planning laws after they move if people always plan to leave a new state. For example, people who move to a new state for years or more for travel, school, projects, or military might keep legal ties to their old state. People often do health care forms for the state a health facility is in. Most immigrants of any kind can do Estate Planning here.

PERSON HAS POWER TO CONTROL THESE THINGS BUT IT'S OFTEN NOT VITAL

Estate Planning to control health care, property, money, children, funeral, and similar things if a person is absent, sick, or dead is usually easy to do because a person legally has full power to control these things. Given this usually judges, doctors, and other people mostly just ask: "Based on what a person wrote what did they likely want done?" It is also easy to do because simple legal documents can do the things and simple words can also be used (like listing some property and putting a few names). Note, despite what many people think often Estate Planning is worth spending a lot on since it often does not greatly change the costs, taxes, delays, and later work in these areas. Benefits seem especially low for young people since only 4% of people die by age 50, and only 0.2% of children before age 18 have both parents die to need legal help. *See Social Security Standard Tables by Felicitie Bell; Parent Mortality Census SIPP Study Paper #288.* Many people spend more energy and money on getting good life insurance to help the people they love.

BOOK IS SHORT, HAS FORMS TO QUICKLY SEE, AND USES EMPHASIS

This book is short and may read rough but can be read fast. Long books often lead to misunderstanding of the basics and skimming. This book has legal forms people can quickly see. For emphasis paragraph titles, underlining, and boxes are used. This book capitalizes some legal words like Will, Testator, and Agent but this is optional. To save space some small words are skipped and end quote marks put before punctuation.

THIS BOOK COVERS MAIN LEGAL IDEAS AND SHOULD SUIT MOST PEOPLE

This book covers the main U.S. legal ideas on Estate Planning and major ways New Jersey law is different. This book can't cover all legal issues but should suit most people without some strange situations or wishes. Strange situations or wishes that may need research or a lawyer include: a) strange gift wishes for property and money, b) wealth over $5 million, c) big medical concerns like extreme age, d) property or money going to a person with a disability or special needs, and e) wish to move or hide assets to qualify for government help.

LEGAL FORMS CAN HELP MANY AND THIS BOOK HAS STANDARD FORMS

Legal forms are good at most things involved in Estate Planning and can make binding legal documents. Instead of legal forms a lawyer can be used for Estate Planning but this can be costly, take months of work, and they can make mistakes. In life people often pick a cheaper option. Importantly, often a hospital, charity, state agency, or state legislature has made a form most people use and call the "standard form", and doctors, judges, and other people may not like to follow anything else. This book does provide mostly standard forms.

LEGAL DOCUMENTS MAY NEED TO BE WITNESSED OR NOTARIZED

To be legally enforceable certain legal documents need to be "witnessed", which is someone watching the person doing the form sign and then the witness signs too. Some documents to be enforceable need to be "notarized" which means a person who is a "notary" sees it signed and then uses an ink stamp and signs. Notaries (also called a "notary public") are at some banks, brokers, insurance agents, courts, law offices, libraries, and mailing-copying centers. Using a phonebook to call to find a notary willing to help is common. The words "subscribe" and "execute" means a person signed a document, and "acknowledgment" means a person said a signature was theirs. If a person signs a document in a foreign language it is usually binding. When filling in a form it may help people to know "respectively" in a form means "in the order just stated". When filling out a legal form except for signatures the other parts can be filled in by a person not doing a form and using pencil is even allowed for this. Once done often people try to keep the original document and hand out copies. Some people have everyone sign multiple copies to have many copies with ink signatures.

SOME LESS COMMON OR LESS USEFUL FORMS ARE NOT IN THIS BOOK

This book skips some possible but less common or less useful documents.

- A "Codicil" can modify a Will but it is easier and legally safer to just rewrite the whole Will.

- Some people do a "Pet Trust" to help a pet, but it's easier to just give money in Will to person given a pet.

- Some people do a "Revocable Living Trust" so a Trust entity with a Trustee holds property or money during their life, usually done to after death have faster transfer of things and avoid small delays, costs, or work of others (by "avoiding probate"). But this is rarely done as it may require moving most of a person's things to a Trust causing maybe years of hassle, mostly to avoid later small work for people happy to be getting things.

- "Childrens Trust" papers can be done (like as part of a Will) so at a death a Trust gets money or property for a minor child to manage until 18, but this is uncommon due to possible cost and hassle, since it rarely matters (as this book explains), and since most Wills already arrange other legal help for young children.

- Though separate forms exist usually organ donation in handled in drivers license or state ID paperwork.

USUALLY NO FEDERAL OR NEW JERSEY TAX IS OWED DUE TO A DEATH

Usually no federal tax is owed due to a death, including no estate, inheritance, or death taxes, since the "Federal Estate And Gift Tax" only starts when a tax credit is used up that covers $13.61 million a person in 2024 (with expected yearly rises for inflation).

New Jersey in 2018 canceled its "Estate Tax" directly on a person who dies or their estate, but left a small "Inheritance Tax" on people getting things by Will or other way at a death which varies by "class".

■ People in "Inheritance Tax Class A" are not taxed and includes most family including spouse (or civil partner), parent, grandparent, child (natural, adopted, or step), grandchild, great-grandchild, and charities.

■ "Inheritance Tax Class C" is decedent's brother or sister, and decedent's child's spouse or civil union partner, and for them the first $25,000 is tax free and after this a 15-16% tax applies.

■ "Inheritance Class D" is everyone else and then on amounts over $500 a 15%-16% tax applies.

Basically, in most cases, close family face no taxes upon a death but a friend may face just 15% or so.

CHAPTER 2
TERMS, PROPERTY LAW, AND HELPFUL INFORMATION FORM

THERE ARE BASIC TERMS AND IDEAS IN ESTATE PLANNING
Some legal terms and ideas are basic to Estate Planning.

■ "Estate Planning" is about people doing legal documents to control things if later absent, sick, or dead. After a document is done people are mostly free to sell or transfer property, instruct doctors, or change forms.

■ A "person doing a legal document" and "doing a form" means the form is for and affects that person.

■ "Probate" is a legal process to do things after someone's death like transfer property, handle creditors, and authorize a Guardian. Due to changes in the law probate is now often informal, faster, and less costly.

■ A "Will" or "will" (this book uses upper case "W") is a legal document done to control issues after death. The phrase "Last Will And Testament" is used since a "Testament" long ago was a small document done along with a Will to do some things.

■ A person doing a Will is called "Testator" or "Will maker". Before about 1995 a woman Testator was called a "Testatrix" and woman Executor called an "Executrix" but this is no longer often said or written.

■ If no valid Will is done a person is "intestate" and then a dead person's property and money is transferred to a spouse, children, and family as intestate law says. <u>Some people a fine with this</u>. This is covered later.

■ A person who died is called the "decedent" or "deceased". A person getting a Will gift is called a "recipient", "beneficiary", or "heir" if related (they "inherit"). "Survive" or "surviving" is to be alive after someone else died. The term "descendants" or "issue" usually means a person's children and grandchildren.

■ A person named in a Will to handle things after someone's death is called an "Executor", but if a judge has to pick someone they are called an "Administrator". <u>The new term "Personal Representative" covers both these things and this new term is now commonly used in most Wills in New Jersey</u>.

■ Legally property is: 1) "real property" which is land and buildings ("real estate"), 2) "fixtures" which are things tied to real property (like fences, carpets, and wired-in appliances), or 3) "personal property" which is everything else (like household items, clothes, tools, cars, jewelry, art, moneys, accounts, and stocks),

■ A person under 18 is usually called a "minor" and often a parent or guardian helps them do things. A minor or other person not reasonably able to make wise decisions lacks "capacity" and is "incapacitated".

■ A document giving power to someone is often called a "Power of Attorney" where the "Principal" gives power to someone called the "Agent" or "Attorney-in-Fact" (but they needn't be a real attorney or a lawyer).

■ State law is the New Jersey Statutes, sometimes called "revised" or "annotated". Each law is called a "statute" or "section" shown by a "§" or "s" mark. A form put in law for people to find and use if wanted is called a "statutory form". An example of one way to cite a New Jersey law is: "N.J. Statutes § 3B:3-1".

ESTATE MEANS PROPERTY OF DECEDENT AND ENTITY HOLDING THINGS
The "estate" or "probate estate" means <u>all property and money of a dead person</u> that at death or soon after didn't automatically legally go to new owners. Estate is also the <u>name for a temporary entity run by an Executor to do things after a death</u> (it's like a small corporation, e.g., "Estate of John Alan Smith").

PERSON CAN ONLY GIFT IN WILL WHAT THEY OWN AT DEATH
A person can only gift by Will things they own at death, <u>so people should research what they do own</u>. Basically by law a person usually owns all they earn as wages and salary, owns their share of income and profit tied to property they own, and owns or partly owns any things their money buys or improves. And for property with "title" documents (real estate or vehicles) or where there is a "listed owner" (like accounts) the named persons are usually the legal owners unless evidence shows special circumstances. Note, a person during life can sell property, make gifts, or transfer things even if they are named in a Will, so <u>people should consider if they already sold or gave away property they also name in a Will gift</u>.

THINGS OWNED IN SPECIAL WAYS MAY LIMIT GIFTING IN WILL
A person should consider if they own real estate or other property in special ownership ways which may limit gifting by Will. Laws vary in different states but <u>some common special ways of ownership are</u>:

- "joint tenant with right of survivorship" or similar legal options is used in papers, so at a death property goes automatically to other named owners despite what a Will says (this in often how spouses hold a home);
- papers say a "life estate" exists, so then if life of someone ends the other people in papers get item; and
- "Trust property" occurs if paperwork made a Trust entity and then property was transferred into it or this is set to occur, so then the Trust papers control where things put in the Trust go after someone's death.

Simple "joint ownership" with many owners can occur if people do joint papers, all agree to it, buy with joint funds, or if a gift was to many people. Wills <u>can</u> gift joint property, like "I give my half of boat to Ed Hu".

NON-PROBATE TRANSFERS THAT HAPPEN AUTOMATICALLY IGNORE A WILL
It is vital to be aware <u>some money or property of a decedent may automatically transfer on death</u> or soon after to new owners <u>if certain arrangements were made earlier</u>. This is usually called "non-probate property". Such things transfer as arranged even if a Will names the same items in Will gifts.

Examples are: a) a "designated beneficiary" form was done to name people to get an investment or account, b) transfer-on-death accounts were used, and c) real property is held by 2 people as "joint tenants with survivorship" or similar so at a death the surviving person gets things. Also, usually property in a Trust will ignore a Will and transfer as Trust papers say to. Life insurance usually goes to the named beneficiary.

Trying to do non-probate transfers for all things is called "avoiding probate", but few people try this since it can cause years of hassle, benefits are small, and often some thing is missed. <u>When doing a Will people should consider non-probate transfers that will occur automatically at a death and consider what will be left</u>.

HELPFUL INFORMATION FORM CAN HELP TELL FAMILY AND FRIENDS THINGS
<u>People can do an unofficial "Helpful Information" form</u> banks, lawyers, and planners suggest so family or friends after a death will know things. People can staple records or lists to this. <u>See form on next pages</u>.

ESTATE PLANNING HELPFUL INFORMATION

For more space attach copies of form or blank pages. Keep pages by Will or other place for Executor or family.

1. Personal Information (Name, Birthdate, Social Security number, special family details, other):

2. Real estate, vehicles, and other major tangible property (especially if people may not find them):

3. Non-tangible assets like stocks, accounts, investments, loans owed you, and business interests:

4. Possible income or insurance like pensions, retirement, disability, insurance, or contracts:

5. Debts owed by you like credit card, loan, student loan, mortgage, car loans, and accounts payable:

6. Names and information of professionals used (attorneys, accountants, brokers, doctors, others):

7. Computer passwords and helpful files, document places, and safes or safe-deposit boxes code/key:

8. Other helpful things, wishes for funeral, special requests, and last messages to family and friends:

CHAPTER 3
WILL BASICS

WILL LETS A PERSON CONTROL THINGS AFTER THEIR DEATH
A Will is a legal document done by a person to control some things after their death. A person doing a Will is called the "Testator" or "Will maker". In New Jersey a Testator when signing must be at least age 18, of sound mind (rational with sufficient memory), and not be under duress (unfair pressure or threat).

KEEP SIGNED WILL IN SAFE PLACE IT CAN BE FOUND AFTER A DEATH
A Will should be kept so it can be found within days of a death, like in a desk, drawer, safe, with a person, or less often a safe deposit box. It may help to tell family how to get a Will. In New Jersey a Will may not be filed before a person's death. The New Jersey Secretary of State does run a "Will Registry" where people can file a 1 page form to just say where family and friend after a death can find a Will, but few people use this.

A WILL USUALLY MUST BE SIGNED WITH 2 WITNESSES
WILL MUST SHOW IT'S A WILL AND USUALLY BE SIGNED WITH 2 WITNESSES
In New Jersey a document to be a Will must show it is a Will by its words, and the person doing it usually must sign in front of 2 persons acting as witnesses who then sign too. A Will just spoken on a video or audio recording usually has no legal effect. As this book later covers New Jersey does let witnesses be skipped if a Will is all handwritten. Some people modify a Will to have 3 or 4 witnesses just in case this may help later.

WITNESSES SHOULD AT LEAST AGE 18 AND OFTEN NOT GETTING WILL GIFTS
A person to witness a Will must be at least age 18. It is best but not legally required a witness not be very old, live far away, or be named in a Will to be Executor, Guardian, or similar. In New Jersey unlike some states a Will is still valid if a witness is getting Will gifts. But many people just to avoid the appearance of misconduct pick witnesses who are "disinterested" which means they or their spouse are not named to get things in a Will. Often people used as witnesses are friends, neighbors, strangers, or family.

TESTATOR AND 2 WITNESSES SIGN THE WILL WHEN TOGETHER IN 1 ROOM
A person doing a Will usually signs it with at least 2 witnesses who also sign while all are in 1 room and see others sign. People showing others an ID is not required but is common. A Testator need not initial the Will pages. A Testator or witness usually use their full legal name unless they dislike and rarely use it. Witnesses only read the 1 paragraph they sign. Some Wills have each witness print their name and address. Legally a Testator needn't say anything but often they say a thing like, "My name is ____ this is my Will that I do voluntarily and ask you 2 people to witness". Lawyers call a person saying aloud a document is their Will as "publishing a Will". Some Testators chat about a Will with witnesses to help show they are of sound mind.

CANCELING OLD WILLS IS USUALLY NOT A PROBLEM
So a new Will is followed old Wills should be canceled ("revoked") but this is easy and rarely a problem. A new Will usually quickly says old Wills are revoked to cancel them, and all this book's Will forms say this. Or people can revoke an old Will by writing "void" or "cancelled" or "X" on it, preferably with a witness to this. Usually crossing out just part of a Will has no effect. Revoking a Will usually doesn't bring back an earlier Will.

OFTEN AT START OF A WILL A PERSON NAMES ANY SPOUSE AND CHILDREN

Many Wills start with a place for a Testator to name any current living spouse and children of any age. Natural or adopted children should be put here including any born outside marriage. People without this family can skip this or put "none". Not doing this may invalidate a Will by indicating a person lacks sufficient mental ability, or let a spouse or child not listed ask a judge to give them a share or all of the estate by claiming a Testator just forgot them. After listing family in a Will a Testator is often free to give them nothing.

MOST WILLS SAY TO LATER SKIP BOND AND ALSO DO INFORMAL PROBATE

Most Wills helpfully say no "bond" or "surety" is required for any Executor, Guardian, or similar person. A bond is insurance from a company to insure against misconduct. A Testator usually doesn't want a bond since the persons Testator names are trusted and them later needing a bond will cost the estate money. Also, most Wills say later the family and friends may do "informal probate" which can avoid costs and delays. Informal probate often is done with just 1 court hearing and often is completed in well under 1 year.

MOST WILLS HAVE A MISCELLANEOUS PART WITH HELPFUL LANGUAGE

Most Wills have a "Miscellaneous" page with paragraphs of legal language to avoid some legal problems. This can help if later legal problems occur. A person doing a Will need not understand these paragraphs.

A WILL NAMES AN EXECUTOR TO DO THINGS AFTER DEATH

A WILL NAMES SOMEONE TO BE EXECUTOR TO DO THINGS AFTER A DEATH

Usually a Will names someone as "Executor" to act after a death. The law gives Executors many helpful legal powers, like to handle debts, find and collect and give new owners property and money, and do probate If a Will fails to name an Executor a judge can pick someone, but family may argue about who to suggest. Note, the term "Personal Representative" and not Executor is now often used in New Jersey for the person doing things after a death, but these terms mostly mean the same thing. Will gifts can go to an Executor.

EXECUTOR CAN BE PAID AND ESTATE PAYS FOR EXECUTOR'S EXPENSES

New Jersey law says a person can ask to can be paid for their work as Executor, and state law has a fee schedule which is complex but basically gives an Executor 3.5% of the estate. See N.J. Statutes § 3B:18-14. In actual practice most Executors later skip asking for pay so as to not owe income tax and leave more resources in the estate to carry out Will gifts. Note, expenses an Executor has like for insurance, utilities, repairs, funeral, mortgage, attorneys, and probate costs are paid for with money or property of the estate. Any lawyer an Executor hires usually is paid hourly or a fixed sum that the lawyer and Executor agree on.

EXECUTOR IS PERSON AT LEAST 18 AND SECOND PERSON RARELY NEEDED

A person to be Executor must be at least age 18 and usually not have a bad criminal record like a felony. A person not residing in New Jersey can be Executor but being local makes work easier. Naming 2 people to both be Executor is allowed but rare due to the risk of arguments and delays, and since any 1 person named should be trusted. People can name a 2nd person to be Executor if the 1st person is not later available but most skip this since this rarely occurs and if needed a judge can always just pick someone. To add such a 2nd person a person could add: "or if they're reasonably unable to serve I name ___ to serve".

CHAPTER 4
WILL GIFTS INCLUDING RESIDUE CLAUSE

MAIN USE OF A WILL IS TO WRITE GIFTS TO HAPPEN AFTER DEATH

Most people use a Will mainly to legally say what happens to their property and money after their death, usually by writing down various Will gifts to occur when they die. Verbal and even writings about this are not usually valid if not in a written Will. A Will can control property acquired after it was signed. The end of this Chapter covers "intestate law" which says where a person's things go at death if no valid Will handles this.

GIFTING IN A WILL USING SIMPLE WORDS OFTEN IS BEST

Making gifts in a Will using simple words is often best, using words like "I give to" and "I gift to". This is legally fine and avoids confusing legal words like "bequest", "devise", and "legacy" which few people know.

A PERSON IS MOSTLY FREE TO GIFT THEIR THINGS AS WANTED

A person is mostly free to give at death their money and property as they want. But creditors a decedent owed money, a spouse, and minor children under age 18 may have some rights which this book later covers.

IN WILL CAN DO SPECIFIC GIFTS TO GIFT PARTICULAR PROPERTY

Most Wills have "specific gifts" to gift particular things. Specific gifts can be any property, like "I give boat to Ed Blom" and "I give UBank account #84553873 to Sue Wu". If a gift is not clear the law assumes all of a kind of thing is given, like "I give jewelry to Ann Po" means all jewelry. But gifting specific property can have surprises like value of items can change, or a Will gift may later fail to occur if property is not owned at death.

IN WILL CAN DO GENERAL GIFTS LIKE OF MONEY

Wills can do "general gifts" where what is gifted is not particular property but can be flexibly chosen, like "I give 1 of my 3 cars to Ed Po" which lets an Executor pick which car. The usual general gift is money, like "I give $5 to Ed Hu". Money gifts are easy to write, let equal gifts be made, and are legally safer for many reasons. To carry out money gifts an Executor usually uses accounts or sells some property in the estate.

RESIDUE CLAUSE IS CATCH-ALL THAT HELPFULLY GIFTS ANYTHING LEFT

Most Wills by their end have a Residue Clause to gift property or money not already gifted in a Will or used other ways, often called a "catch-all" or "left-over" clause. This is covered later in this Chapter.

PERSON IN WILL GIFT USUALLY MUST SURVIVE OR GIFT DOES NOT OCCUR

Many Wills like this book's Will forms say a person named in a Will gift must survive (live past) the Testator for the gift to occur unless gift language specifically says different. If survival is not required for a Will gift what happens if a named recipient is dead can be unclear (state laws can be very complex). People doing a Will should consider how Will gifts to people dying before Testator usually have no effect. People if they see a person in a Will gift has died can re-do a Will or just let the Residue Clause handle it.

CONDITIONS ON WILL GIFTS ARE RARE DUE TO POSSIBLE PROBLEMS

Putting conditions on a gift, like "I give Ann Poe $90 if she graduates college", can cause problems like years of delay, risk of lawsuits, and big attorney's fees. Due to all this conditions are rarely put on Will gifts.

PROPERTY OR MONEY IN A JOINT GIFT GOES TO MULTIPLE PEOPLE

The same property or money in a "joint gift" can go to many people to each get a part. For example, "I give boat and all hats to Ann Baxter and Mary Ann Swanson" means each person owns part of every item. People later can split things by agreement or an Executor can decide how to divide items. If a person in a joint gift has died their part usually is left to transfer under a Residue Clause.

PEOPLE CAN ADD AN ALTERNATE BENEFICIARY LIKE FOR SPECIAL ITEMS

A person named in a Will gift dying before a Testator is rare, and if seen people can re-do a Will to name new persons or let a Will's Residue Clause handle it. Some people to prepare for this chance maybe for special items write an "alternate beneficiary", like "I give boat to Ed Liu but if they don't survive me to Ann Liu".

CAN SAY IF PERSON IN GIFT DIES THEN IT GOES TO LINEAL DESCENDANTS

A Will gift can say it goes to a person but if they don't survive then to their "lineal descendants per stirpes". Descendants are a person's children and grandchildren. "Per stirpes" means "by branch" and is about how to spread property and money, and it mostly tries to divide things so each family branch gets an equal share. Most Wills use "lineal descendants" language in a Residue Clause. An example shows how it works:

A Will may say: **"Clothes to Sue Wu but if they don't survive to their lineal descendants per stirpes"**, and this means if Sue Wu has died and her son Ken Wu is living and her other son Ben Wu has died but left 2 children then, legally, under the law Ken Wu himself gets 50% and Ben Wu's 2 children each get 25%.

GIFT BENEFICIARIES CAN GET PERCENTAGE RATHER THAN EQUAL SHARE

If a Will gift goes to multiple people the law assumes equal shares, but if wanted percentages can be used to make unequal gifts, like "I give boat 90% to John Smith and 10% to Mary Baker".

GIFTS IN WILL CAN GO TO A GROUP OR CLASS OF PEOPLE

To save work a Will gift can go to a group or class of people like certain family if who is meant is later easy to determine. People can say roughly how much in total is gifted to be clearer. Examples are: "I give $10 to each person on my 2018 soccer team" and "I give $10 to each of my grandkids so this is about $100 in total."

AFTER A DEATH FAMILIES OFTEN LET PEOPLE TAKE ITEMS UNOFFICIALLY

Many families unofficially let people take items in ways a dead person said, showed by stickers, or wrote on a note, which is often fine. If anyone objects a judge often has the Will and law be followed fully but later people can voluntarily retransfer items. Later this book explains gifts done by Tangible Personal Property Memorandum.

LATER DIVORCE OR MURDER CANCELS WILL GIFTS

New Jersey law says a person divorcing or murdering a Testator usually cancels Will gifts to the person.

PROBABLY DO NEW DOCUMENTS IF DIVORCE, MARRY, HAVE CHILD, OR MOVE

Divorcing, marrying, having a new child, or moving to a new state can have big legal effects, and if any of these events occur it is recommended people do a new Will and other Estate Planning papers soon. To help most states say a Will from another state is still valid if people move but this is not always certain.

RESIDUE CLAUSE GIFTING ALL LEFT IS MAIN WAY USED TO GIFT THINGS

THE RESIDUE CLAUSE IS CATCH-ALL THAT HELPS GIFT ANYTHING LEFT

Most Wills by their end have a Residue Clause to gift any property or money not gifted earlier in a Will or used in other ways. Things transferred this way is called the "Residue". Many people gift most their money and property this way by intentionally not mentioning in a Will most things so the Residue Clause handles it. This avoids need to describe things and has less legal risk. After applying a Residue Clause if anything is somehow left then by law a decedent's closest heirs-at-law get things (this is their closest family).

USUAL RESIDUE CLAUSE HAS 2 PARTS

A short 2 part Residue Clause is usual and is used in this book's Will forms, and it has:

1) 1st space to name 1 or more persons to get things if they survive Testator (many name a spouse or closest family here), and if several people are named but only some survive then survivors split things, and

2) 2nd space to name persons to get things if all in the 1st space don't survive (many people name next close family or friends in this space), and if a person in 2nd space has died their descendants get their share.

EXAMPLE OF 2 PART RESIDUE CLAUSE:

"RESIDUE CLAUSE: I give money and property not gifted earlier, the residue:
   a) to   John Paul Doe my husband   who survive me with persons just named who survive me taking the share of non-survivors, then if anything remains
   b) to   Sam Doe, Beth Wu, and Greta Fisher   and if any of those just named do not survive me their part goes to their lineal descendants per stirpes."

In this example if John Paul Doe has survived he gets all things, but if John Paul Doe hasn't survived and also Sam Doe hasn't survived and he left 2 daughters then those 2 daughters split the 1/3 share of his (so get 1/6 each) and the other 2 persons in the second part Beth Wu and Greta Fisher get 1/3 each.

A FEW PEOPLE REWRITE RESIDUE CLAUSE TO HAVE 1 PART

A normal Residue Clause of 2 parts is often fine for most people. But a few people modify a Will to have a "1 Part Residue Clause" since it tends to gift to a group more equally and be simpler to understand. People with no spouse and no young children are likelier to do this change, but even they often don't bother. See Example below for exact words to use if people want to change to a 1 Part Residue Clause.

EXAMPLE OF 1 PART RESIDUE CLAUSE:

"RESIDUE CLAUSE: The rest, residue, and remainder of my estate, property of any kind and nature, and anything I have an interest in, I give to Adam Doe and Beth Wu who survive me and to lineal descendants per stirpes of any person just named who did not survive me."

In this example if Adam hasn't survived but had 2 children they each get 25%, and if Beth Wu survived she gets 50%. Or if Beth Wu also hadn't survived and had 5 kids they split her part and each gets 10%.

CAN LEAVE SOME WILL GIFT LINES BLANK OR WRITE TO SAY SKIP

A person writing a Will can choose to not use some gifts lines in a Will legal form, like by just leaving them blank, writing things like "SKIPPED" or "NONE" in them, or using a computer to delete some gift lines. Judges and others usually do not care about neatness or empty spaces in Wills.

MUST SUFFICIENTLY DESCRIBE NAMES AND PROPERTY IN A WILL

PUTTING NAMES OF PEOPLE OR GROUPS IN A WILL IS FAIRLY EASY

Putting names in Wills is fairly easy. <u>A judge or Executor assume a person in a Will meant people they know, so common names are OK unless 2 friends or family have the same name</u>. Details can help if names won't be recognized or to be friendly, like "I give $5 to my nurse Sue Ax" and "I give $5 to loyal pal Ed Lee". If people used a nickname "also known as" or "a/k/a" may help, like "I give $5 to Dan Smith a/k/a Old Fishy". Gifts can go to a charity, government, or group, like "I give $10 to The Salvation Army, "I give $8 to Trenton Public Library, New Jersey", and "I give $5 to Wix Church, Rex, TX". People can phone for a charity's name.

PUTTING DESCRIPTIONS OF ITEMS IN WILL GIFTS IS FAIRLY EASY

Describing items in gifts is easy since people rarely own similar items. Often fine are gifts like: "I give ax to Ed Wu" and "I give big table to Ann Fox". It's OK to gift by category or list, like: "I give tools to Sam Lee" and "I give cow, van, and harp to Sue Hill". Financial assets can use plain words, like "bank accounts" or "stocks", but details can help, like: "US Bank account ending #1511". <u>Gifting using a location is riskier</u> as judges will ignore Will gifts if it seems items were placed to affect gifting and no "independently significant" life reason. So, "I give Ed Po items in safe and desk" judges might not follow, but "I give Ed Po hats in attic" likely is OK.

DESCRIBING REAL PROPERTY IS HARD IF NOT USING RESIDUE OR TITLE

The easier, legally safer way to transfer real property (real estate) at death is: 1) do nothing specific so it's handled by a Will Residue Clause, or 2) have a lawyer or agent put names in a deed or similar document so then named persons legally get things at someone's death. Most use these 2 ways to transfer real property.

Gifting real property other ways is harder though possible. Helpfully a Will gift of real property <u>described by location</u> legally does gift <u>all land, buildings, and fixtures located there</u> with no need to describe what's there.

It is possible to <u>gift real property at a particular address with very plain words</u>, like a house, fixtures, and land can be fully given by something like: "I give 81 Maxwell Street, Camden, New Jersey, to Mary Ann Brown".

People can do a <u>blanket gift</u> giving all of a kind of property, like, "I give all real property and fixtures in Bergen County, New Jersey to Ann Ivy Hill " or "I give all furniture and all bank accounts to Eric Paul Carlson".

Giving real property in a Will using a "legal description" is how many lawyers do it, but this can be hard to do. If using a legal description people must copy without mistakes <u>the full legal description of maybe many lines</u> into a Will with no abbreviation at all. A legal description might be found on a deed or on mortgage papers. Legal descriptions may refer to a "lot" or "blocks" on a map which is recorded in land records of a county, or it may refer to a path around the land borders with various angles, distances, and iron stakes.

MOST STATES AND WILLS SAY PEOPLE TO GET GIFTS MUST SURVIVE 5 DAYS

Helpful laws in most states and all this book's Will forms say if a person dies within 5 days (120 hours) or simultaneously with a Testator, then they are legally seen as dying before Testator. This skips the need to prove exact time of death (like if people die in 1 accident), and avoids a Will gift or right to something going to someone who then soon dies within days (so an item may have to go through multiple probate proceedings).

SIMPLE WILL WITH MOST GIFTING DONE BY RESIDUE CLAUSE IS OFTEN BEST

Writing a simple Will without many gifts, much left blank, and mostly using a Residue Clause is often best.

If there is no spouse and no children often a person does a few small gifts, and then names some family or friends in the Residue Clause to get everything remaining.

If there is only a spouse often a person does small gifts to friends and family, then uses the Residue Clause of the Will to gift all left to the spouse, and then names a few fallback persons in the Residue Clause.

A parent with young children if married to the other parent often does small gifts to friends and family, then in the Residue Clause gives mostly to a spouse, and then names children as fallbacks in the Residue Clause.

A parent with young children if not married or close to the other parent often does small gifts to friends and family, and then uses the Residue Clause to gift all remaining to the children.

INTESTATE LAW COVERS PROPERTY OR MONEY NOT HANDLED BY WILL

INTESTATE LAW CONTROLS THINGS NOT HANDLED BY A WILL OR SIMILAR

State "intestate" law at New Jersey Statutes § 3B:5-3 and § 3B:5-4 says if a person dies with no valid Will or if anything is left after Will and transfers are done then some surviving (living) family get the money and property left by the person who died (their "estate"). The legal term "intestate" means to not have a Will. Many people like who intestate law transfers things to and choose to skip a Will, but often doing a Will has some other benefits. Note, the term "descendants" means a person's children and grandchildren, and if someone has died who would have got an intestate share often their descendants legally get that share. New Jersey intestate law if it applies basically says, in order, the following:

1) if decedent (the person who died) left some surviving (living) descendants but no surviving spouse, then the descendants get all of the estate of decedent;

2) if decedent left a surviving spouse and either a) no descendants, or b) all of decedent's descendants are shared with the spouse and the spouse has no other descendants, then the spouse gets all the estate;

3) if decedent left a surviving spouse and also a) surviving children of the decedent or the spouse who are not all shared with the other, or b) surviving parents, then the spouse gets a certain minimum amount and then about half of the estate and then the remainder goes to either decedent's children or parents;

4) if decedent left no surviving spouse or descendants then things go to decedent's next nearest relatives starting with decedent's parents, then brothers and sisters, then cousins, and then other close family; and

5) if none of the above persons survive, then the decedent's estate goes to the state of New Jersey.

CHAPTER 5
DEBT, MARRIAGE, AND YOUNG CHILD ISSUES

THIS CHAPTER COVERS CERTAIN ISSUES THAT SOME PEOPLE CAN SKIP
This Chapter covers debt, marriage, and young child issues, and some people can skip parts of this.

DEBT ISSUES

PAYING DECEDENT'S DEBTS MAY USE UP RESOURCES AND REDUCE GIFTS
If a decedent had debts then creditors owed may ask a judge to be paid from decedent's money or property before Will gifts and certain transfers occur. How debts are paid is set by state law and a Will need not describe this. Funds to pay debts comes from decedent's money and property so may affect (in order) the Will Residue, Will general gifts, Will specific gifts, and non-probate transfers. Probate, health care, taxes, and funeral costs by law have some priority to be paid first. For certain reasons often not all debts are paid. People should consider how paying debts may use up money or property, leaving less to carry out Will gifts. A spouse and family usually aren't liable for decedent's debts unless they actually guaranteed or co-signed.

SECURED DEBTS LIKE MORTGAGE OR VEHICLE LIEN ARE NOT PAID OFF
Laws in most states say do not pay off secured debts on property of a decedent like a house mortgage or vehicle lien even if other debts are paid by Executor or in probate. This avoids using up estate resources on paying these usually big debts and leaves more estate resources to carry out Will gifts and other transfers. Due to this, all this book's Will forms say do not usually pay off any secured debts. But if a Testator wants they can 1) put in a Will an order to pay (like, "Executor pay off the house mortgage"), or 2) gift enough money to pay off a secured debt to the person getting the property. Most banks let the new owners after a death keep paying monthly any secured debt like a mortgage or lien.

FAMILY RIGHTS MAY BE USED TO GET FAMILY THINGS BEFORE DEBTS
Most states have "Family Rights" a decedent's surviving spouse or children can claim, and this helpfully may let them get things even before most debts of decedent are paid and even before Will gifts.

First, in many U.S. states a surviving spouse or if there is no spouse then decedent's children can use an "Exempt Property" right to get ownership of some of a decedent's clothing and household items to use to live. In New Jersey the Exempt Property right amount is $5,000 in 2024. See N.J. Statutes § 3B:16-5. Often family can keep even more of decedent's items by claiming the decedent gifted them more things.

Second, in many U.S. states a surviving spouse and young children can use a "Family Allowance" right to get some of a decedent's money and property to live on for 1 year or so. In New Jersey a spouse can use this right to get money from the estate to live on during any long probate proceeding. See N.J. Statutes § 3B:3-30.

Third, in many U.S. states if a decedent left a small estate the family can use a "Small Estate Affidavit" to get most of what there is. New Jersey does this, and here a surviving spouse can use an affidavit to get all a decedent left if there is under $50,000 of money and property. Or if there is no spouse then a child can use an affidavit to get all that is left if there is under $20,000 of money and property. See N.J. Statutes § 3B:10-3.

Fourth, in many states a surviving spouse or young children have some right to get (or stay in for years) the house or mobile home owned by a decedent under a "Homestead Law". But New Jersey law mostly does not say a spouse or children by law automatically get the homestead property. Instead New Jersey law just says if a spouse or children of decedent get the house by some means then creditors of the decedent can't usually seek payment by involving the house. Of course any mortgages already on a house usually must be paid. No matter what a spouse or children living in a home may be legally and practically very hard to remove. So family don't try to cause legal trouble about a house usually a person gives a house mostly to a spouse or young children. Some people may want to do other research.

MARRIAGE ISSUES

NEW JERSEY USES SEPARATE PROPERTY LAW FOR SPOUSES

New Jersey like most states uses the Separate Property Law system that says a married person mostly owns their money and property separately and not jointly with a spouse. Due to this a married person is usually free to sell during life or gift by Will most of their money or property and not have to involve a spouse. But joint ownership by 2 spouses and not separate ownership can arise in other ways, like by agreement, both spouses paying part of the purchase price, if a gift was to both spouses, or if paperwork calls it joint.

COMMUNITY PROPERTY LAW APPLIES IN OTHER STATES FOR SPOUSES

There are 9 states mostly in the Western U.S. that use the Community Property Law system for spouses (Arizona, California, Louisiana, Idaho, Nevada, New Mexico, Texas, Washington, and Wisconsin). This says property or money is owned 50/50 by spouses as Community Property if it's from mental or physical work while married (like wages or salary) or if items are bought or improved with any other Community Property. People recently moving from these states may face legal issues.

JOINT WILL OR SIMILAR BOTH SPOUSES SIGN IS NOT RECOMMENDED

Some couples who worry a lot try to sign a "Joint Will" or a "Contract To Make A Will" done by a lawyer which says spouses give all to the other if they die first, then says last living spouse gives to all children equally, and usually says a spouse may not change this. This is banned in some states and is rarely used.

SPOUSE CAN CLAIM ELECTIVE SHARE INSTEAD OF THEM FOLLOWING WILL

A spouse if unhappy with what a Will and other transfers may give them has a right to instead choose (elect) an "Elective Share" of a percentage of a dead spouse's property and money rather than take what a Will says. States do this for fairness, so a spouse has resources to live on, and so early divorce isn't the only way to be financially secure. To avoid this both spouses have to sign a complex pre-nuptial or a post-nuptial agreement by a lawyer but this can be costly to arrange. New Jersey sets the Elective Share at 1/3 of the property and money of a spouse who died. In some cases an Elective Share can cover things decedent gave away recently or controlled but didn't own. Clearly if a spouse uses an Elective Share to get 1/3 or so of the decedent's money and property this may take so much that it interferes with some other transfers. To avoid a spouse wanting to use the Elective Share most people give over 1/2 of their things to any spouse of theirs.

YOUNG CHILD ISSUES

WILL CAN NAME A GUARDIAN OF THE PERSON TO CARE FOR YOUNG CHILD

If a parent dies with a child under age 18 then any other natural or adopted parent (but not a step-parent) almost always automatically gets control of the child's care (including health care, school, and home issues). This won't occur only if the other parent will be unavailable a long time or is proven unfit in court which is rare. But just in case it is later needed (like later both parents die) a Will often names a healthy and willing relative or friend as "Guardian of the Person" to give this care for a young child.

WILL CAN NAME A GUARDIAN OF THE ESTATE TO MANAGE CHILD'S PROPERTY

Since a child until age 18 can't legally easily control property including money a Will often names a person to be "Guardian of the Estate" to have the job of managing a young child's property and money. Many states call this a "Guardian of Property" or a "Conservator". This person decides each year how to use property and money on a child's needs (like on school, living, and health care) and then usually at age 18 anything left goes to the child. A person paying things for a child can ask to be paid back. A judge often holds a yearly hearing on spending. As a nice 2nd option to avoid work and costs most Wills say an Executor may name a person including themselves as "Custodian" to manage things under the new Uniform Transfers To Minors Act.

MOST WILLS NAME 1 PERSON TO CARE FOR CHILD AND THEIR PROPERTY

This book's Will forms and most parents name the same 1 person to care for a child and also manage a child's property and money. People can change a Will to name different people for the 2 positions, but this is rarely worth it since parents dying is rare, rarely do children get much, a person smart enough to handle a child often can handle money, and naming different people can lead to arguments and even costly lawsuits between people. Will gifts can go to someone named to be a Guardian.

PERSON TO HELP A CHILD MUST BE AT LEAST 18

To be a Guardian for a child in New Jersey a person must be at least age 18 but they needn't reside here. But later usually a judge can't think they are unfit to serve, which usually means no serious criminal felony or a history of abuse or fraud. The choice by the last living parent is usually followed. If no Will names a person for a position or they're unavailable a judge can pick someone, but family may argue about who to suggest. Naming 2 people to act at the same time in the same position is rare since 2 persons may argue and any 1 person named should be smart enough to act alone. In rare cases a married couple is named for the same position but there can be problems if they divorce or disagree. Some Wills add a 2nd person to serve if the 1st person named is later not available, like: "or if they are later unable to serve I name _____ to serve"). But most people skip naming a fallback person since it is rarely needed, if a problem is seen a Will can be redone by a person, and a judge can just pick someone if needed.

NAMING PERSONS TO HELP CHILD RARELY MATTERS

A child under 18 having parents die is rare so parents shouldn't worry much about naming people to help. A good U.S. study looked at 72,240 people under age 18 and found only 2014 had lost 1 parent (so 2.78%) and only 97 had lost 2 parents (so a very small 0.13%). *Parent Mortality Census SIPP Paper #288.*

CHAPTER 6
BASIC IDEAS ABOUT HEALTH CARE FORMS

BASIC IDEAS HELP PEOPLE UNDERSTAND CONTROLLING HEALTH CARE

Some ideas help people understand health care forms.

■ By law people control their own health care by telling doctors and others what they want <u>unless they're "incapacitated"</u> by insufficient ability to a) <u>communicate</u> verbally or by notes, b) be <u>rational</u>, or c) be <u>conscious</u>. In actuality most people keep control of their own health care till death or till no big treatment options remain, but people may worry they may be incapacitated a long time so they want to do health care forms.

■ If an adult 18 or older becomes incapacitated <u>the adult's closest family like spouse or adult child can make emergency decisions</u> but they usually must then rush to a judge to get further power if no legal document gives them full power over health care.

■ In forms a <u>person can be named to have control of health care</u> if needed who is often called "Agent". Forms about control of health care if people are later incapacitated are often called "Advanced Directives".

■ In forms people can give <u>written health care instructions that doctors, family, and Agent must obey</u>.

■ Parents do have power over health care of <u>their children under age 18</u>.

■ Some **young married people** give a spouse power over health care in case they are ever incapacitated. Some **young adults** give this power to parents. **Young people** are less often ill so often skip doing things.

■ Pain relief like pain drugs and comfort care is usually given even if forms say to stop or limit other care.

■ <u>Most people only do a single long health care form</u> that has a spot to give someone power over health care and a spot for instructions (this is often called a "Health Care Power of Attorney" though names vary).

■ For the rare times stopping health care ("pulling the plug") likely matters due to extreme illness or old age:

-- most people do nothing special and trust family or Agent for health care to decide on stopping care based on many factors like pain, cost, hassle, suffering and time of treatment, beliefs, and chances of recovery;

-- a few people do a serious document to say to stop most health care if <u>later</u> doctors decide a person is incapacitated, has an irrevocable terminal condition or likely won't regain good consciousness, and more medical care won't help (this document to stop care is often called a "Living Will" though names vary);

-- a few people do a serious document to <u>starting immediately</u> block certain health care (and this often is called a "Do-Not-Resuscitate" if about resuscitation or called a "Physician's Order" if about many treatments).

CHAPTER 7
FORM 1: WILL (STANDARD)

FORM 1 IS A STANDARD WILL THAT IS FLEXIBLE BUT WITHOUT GUARDIANS

Form 1 is a flexible Will that lets a person control many things after their death. This form has no part about a Guardian so is for someone with no child under age 18. A person doing a Will is called a Testator.

THIS FORM IS A WILL WITH SEVERAL PARTS

The form starts with lines for a person to put their name (a full legal name is best but not required) and place of main residence (most put a county but some put a city). The Will is still valid if people later move.

Paragraph 1, "List Of Spouse And Children", lets a person write the names of any living spouse and children they have, or if none maybe write "none". This helps show a Testator has enough mental ability and memory to do a Will. Not listing a living spouse or child here can let an omitted person ask a judge to give them a share or all of a Testator's property and money by claiming they were accidently forgotten.

Paragraph 2, "Gifts", has many spaces to make either specific gifts of particular property or general gifts like of money. People can delete, copy and paste to add more, or leave blank these gift lines.

Paragraph 3, "Separate Writings", says to follow any separate writings done apart from the Will that gifts tangible personal property in manner allowed by state law.

Paragraph 4, "Residue", has a Residue Clause to say any property and money left after other Will parts and other transfers is to be distributed in the way a person wrote in the blank parts of this paragraph.

Paragraph 5, "Administration", names a person to be Personal Representative to do things after a person's death (in the past the similar term Executor was used in New Jersey for the person doing this).

Paragraph 6, "Miscellaneous", has paragraphs of legal language to help avoid certain legal issues.

Last is a paragraph for Testator to put the date and sign, and a paragraph for 2 witnesses to put the date, sign, and print the addresses they live at.

USUAL RESIDUE CLAUSE HAS 2 PLACES TO NAME PERSONS TO GET THINGS

In a Will "Residue Clause" anything left over after other Will parts is transferred as the clause directs. Many people use a Residue Clause to gift most their things. In this Will form's Residue Clause there is:

1) a 1st space to name 1 or more persons to get the Residue, and if any named here have died before the Will maker then other persons named here in this 1st space take the dead person's share, and

2) a 2nd space to name people to get things if all people named in the 1st space have died, and if any people named in the 2nd space have died their shares go to "lineal descendants" like their children.

People often put in the 1st space a spouse or closest family or friends, and in 2nd space next closest people.

TESTATOR AND 2 WITNESSES WHILE TOGETHER SIGN WILL

This Will after being filled out (except bits intentionally left blank) must be signed by the person doing the Will (the "Testator") in front of at least 2 persons acting as witnesses at least age 18 who then also sign.

LAST WILL AND TESTAMENT

I, _____, of _____, New Jersey, do revoke all prior Wills and testamentary documents and do make, publish, and declare this as my Will. I am of sound mind and under no duress or undue influence and acting voluntarily.

1. LIST OF SPOUSE AND CHILDREN. To help show I am mentally competent and have sufficient memory to make a Will I wish to list any living spouse and living children I now have. I currently have the following living spouse and living children:
_____
_____.

2. GIFTS. I give these gifts in this Will, but to get a gift in this section the recipient must survive me except as otherwise stated below.

I give _____ to _____.
I give _____ to _____.
I give _____ to _____.
I give _____ to _____.
I give _____ to _____.
I give _____ to _____.
I give _____ to _____.
I give _____ to _____.

3. SEPARATE WRITINGS. I may do writings separate from this Will to gift tangible personal property as allowed by state law, and all such writings should be followed. But any such writing not found within 90 days of my death is canceled and has no effect. A gift in such a writing to a person who does not survive me is canceled and has no effect. This Will does not revoke any such writings that now exist.

4. RESIDUE. I give the rest and residue and remainder of my estate, my money and property of any kind and nature, and anything I have an interest in so long as it was not transferred by other Will provisions (all of which is called the "residue"), as follows:
 a) to _____ who survive me with persons just named who survive me taking the share of non-survivors, then if anything remains
 b) to _____ and if any of those just named do not survive me their part goes to their lineal descendants per stirpes.

5. ADMINISTRATION. I name, nominate, and appoint _____ as Personal Representative including for me, my Will, and my estate.

6. MISCELLANEOUS. The following applies to this Will and generally.

    In this Will no part left unfilled is a mistake including spaces in the residue clause.

    The facts support and I want New Jersey state law to apply to this Will and my estate.

    I order that my just debts, funeral and related expenses, and taxes be paid as soon after my death as practical but only those items my Personal Representative chooses to pay.

    Priority of Will gifts of the same type is based on the order they are written.

    The words "give" and "gift" also means a devise, bequest, grant, legacy, or similar.

    I am intentionally not providing by Will or other ways for some family, including I am not providing for some children of mine and also children of a deceased child of mine.

    If a gift Will reasonably mentions survival then survival is an absolute condition and anti-lapse laws or similar provisions have no effect and without survival the gift lapses. Unless a Will gift specifies otherwise if a Will gift goes to multiple recipients if any do not survive me the part to them lapses and instead goes to other surviving recipients.

    No earlier transfer reduces a Will gift unless I usually called it a loan or advancement.

    In this Will any gender or gendered word includes all genders, and the singular includes the plural and vice versa, and "they" can mean a single person or many persons.

    Unless a Will specifically says otherwise a secured debt including a mortgage or lien shall not be paid off including by a Personal Representative or in probate, and a recipient of a Will gift of property takes it subject to debts. Also, no recipient of property who may lose it or who pays to keep it may have my estate or others pay or do exoneration.

    If during my life I disposed of an item in a specific gift then the gift is extinguished.

    I request and authorize any informal, summary, and quick probate or similar action. Any Personal Representative may act independently with no supervision of any court, including independent administration, and with no inventory, appraisal, or other action.

    I give any Personal Representative the a) fullest authority, discretion, and powers allowed by state law, b) power to lease, sell, mortgage, convey, or keep property including real property in a manner and time they deem helpful or proper, and c) authority to settle or pay claims or debts in the time and manner they choose. Any Personal Representative or other fiduciary shall have all powers and authorities conferred by statute or common law in any jurisdiction they may act, including powers and authorities conferred by Chapter 3B of the New Jersey Statutes Annotated including future amendments.

    Any Guardian of any type, Conservator, Custodian, or other person managing a minor's property or money may use or invade the principal and sell property without court action.

    If context permits the terms Personal Representative and Executor and Administrator are interchangeable, Conservator and Guardian of the Estate and Guardian of Property and Custodian are interchangeable, and residue and residuary are interchangeable. Any such person may stand in the place of and have all powers like the others named here.

The residue includes lapsed or failed gifts, insurance paid to the estate, digital assets, inheritances owed me, and all I had power of appointment or testamentary disposition over.

Any Personal Representative may access, manage, delete, modify, transfer, and otherwise control any digital accounts and assets I had any interest in or power over.

Any Personal Representative, Executor, Administrator, Guardian of any type like for a person or estate, Conservator, Custodian, and any other fiduciary under this Will or otherwise shall qualify and serve without bond, surety, security, surety bond, or similar.

If evidence does not show it likely a person survived me by 120 hours (5 days) then for this Will and my estate they shall be deemed in all ways as having died before me.

If part of this Will is by law invalid or unenforceable other provisions remain in effect.

Any Personal Representative may at any time transfer money or property of a minor under age 18 to a Custodian to serve under the New Jersey Uniform Transfers to Minors Act or similar law anywhere, and may pick a person to be Custodian including themselves.

TESTATOR

IN WITNESS WHEREOF, I declare that this instrument is my Will which I make as Testator and I have voluntarily signed on the ___ day of _____, 20___.

_____
Testator signature

WITNESSES

The foregoing instrument was signed by the Testator in our presence and declared by the Testator to be the Testator's Will, and we, the undersigned Witnesses, sign our names hereunto acting to witness the Will at the request and in the presence of the Testator, and in the presence of each other on the ___ day of _____, 20___.

_____   _____
Witness #1 signature   Witness #1 address

_____   _____
Witness #2 signature   Witness #2 address

CHAPTER 8
FORM 2: WILL (GUARDIAN)

FORM 2 IS A WILL WITH GUARDIAN PART FOR PEOPLE WITH YOUNG CHILD

Form 2 is a Will with a Guardian part to be used by a person with a minor child under age 18.

FORM IS A WILL WITH SEVERAL PARTS INCLUDING A GUARDIAN PART

The form starts with lines for a person to put their name (a full legal name is best but not required) and place of main residence (most put a county but some put a city). The Will is still valid if people later move.

Paragraph 1, "List Of Spouse And Children", lets a person write the names of any living spouse and children they have, or if none maybe write "none". This helps show a Testator has enough mental ability and memory to do a Will. Not listing a living spouse or child here can let an omitted person ask a judge to give them a share or all of a Testator's property and money by claiming they were accidently forgotten.

Paragraph 2, "Gifts", has many spaces to make either specific gifts of particular property or general gifts like of money. People can delete, copy and paste to add more, or leave blank these gift lines.

Paragraph 3, "Separate Writings", says to follow any separate writings done apart from the Will that gifts tangible personal property in manner allowed by state law.

Paragraph 4, "Residue", has a Residue Clause to say any property and money left after other Will parts and other transfers is to be distributed in the way a person wrote in the blank parts of this paragraph.

Paragraph 5, "Administration", names a person to be Personal Representative to do things after a person's death (in the past the similar term Executor was used in New Jersey for the person doing this).

<u>**Paragraph 6, "Guardian"**, names a person as Guardian of the Person to care for minor children under 18 if needed (like if both parents die) and Guardian of the Estate to manage property and money of children</u>.

Paragraph 7, "Miscellaneous", has paragraphs of legal language to help avoid certain legal issues.

Last is a paragraph for Testator to put the date and sign, and a paragraph for 2 witnesses to put the date, sign, and print the addresses they live at.

USUAL RESIDUE CLAUSE HAS 2 PLACES TO NAME PERSONS TO GET THINGS

In a Will "Residue Clause" anything left over after other Will parts is transferred as the clause directs. Many people use a Residue Clause to gift most their things. In this Will form's Residue Clause there is:

1) a 1st space to name 1 or more persons to get the Residue, and if any named here have died before the Will maker then other persons named here in this 1st space take the dead person's share, and

2) a 2nd space to name people to get things if all people named in the 1st space have died, and if any people named in the 2nd space have died their shares go to "lineal descendants" like their children.

People often put in the 1st space a spouse or closest family or friends, and in 2nd space next closest people.

TESTATOR AND 2 WITNESSES WHILE TOGETHER SIGN WILL

This Will after being filled out (except bits intentionally left blank) must be signed by the person doing the Will (the "Testator") in front of at least 2 persons acting as witnesses at least age 18 who then also sign.

LAST WILL AND TESTAMENT

I, _____, of _____, New Jersey, do revoke all prior Wills and testamentary documents and do make, publish, and declare this as my Will. I am of sound mind and under no duress or undue influence and acting voluntarily.

1. LIST OF SPOUSE AND CHILDREN. To help show I am mentally competent and have sufficient memory to make a Will I wish to list any living spouse and living children I now have. I currently have the following living spouse and living children:
_____
_____.

2. GIFTS. I give these gifts in this Will, but to get a gift in this section the recipient must survive me except as otherwise stated below.

I give _____ to _____.
I give _____ to _____.
I give _____ to _____.
I give _____ to _____.
I give _____ to _____.
I give _____ to _____.
I give _____ to _____.
I give _____ to _____.

3. SEPARATE WRITINGS. I may do writings separate from this Will to gift tangible personal property as allowed by state law, and all such writings should be followed. But any such writing not found within 90 days of my death is canceled and has no effect. A gift in such a writing to a person who does not survive me is canceled and has no effect. This Will does not revoke any such writings that now exist.

4. RESIDUE. I give the rest and residue and remainder of my estate, my money and property of any kind and nature, and anything I have an interest in so long as it was not transferred by other Will provisions (all of which is called the "residue"), as follows:
  a) to _____ who survive me with persons just named who survive me taking the share of non-survivors, then if anything remains
  b) to _____ and if any of those just named do not survive me their part goes to their lineal descendants per stirpes.

5. ADMINISTRATION. I name, nominate, and appoint _____
as Personal Representative including for me, my Will, and my estate.

6. GUARDIAN. I name, nominate, and appoint _____
to be Guardian of the Person of any minor child of mine and also to have care, authority, custody, and other control of them. I also name this same person to be Guardian of the Estate and Property for any minor child of mine and also to have care, control, and power over their property, money, and estate.

7. MISCELLANEOUS. The following applies to this Will and generally.
    In this Will no part left unfilled is a mistake including spaces in the residue clause.
    The facts support and I want New Jersey state law to apply to this Will and my estate.
    I order that my just debts, funeral and related expenses, and taxes be paid as soon after my death as practical but only those items my Personal Representative chooses to pay.
    Priority of Will gifts of the same type is based on the order they are written.
    The words "give" and "gift" also means a devise, bequest, grant, legacy, or similar.
    I am intentionally not providing by Will or other ways for some family, including I am not providing for some children of mine and also children of a deceased child of mine.
    If a gift Will reasonably mentions survival then survival is an absolute condition and anti-lapse laws or similar provisions have no effect and without survival the gift lapses. Unless a Will gift specifies otherwise if a Will gift goes to multiple recipients if any do not survive me the part to them lapses and instead goes to other surviving recipients.
    No earlier transfer reduces a Will gift unless I usually called it a loan or advancement.
    In this Will any gender or gendered word includes all genders, and the singular includes the plural and vice versa, and "they" can mean a single person or many persons.
    Unless a Will specifically says otherwise a secured debt including a mortgage or lien shall not be paid off including by a Personal Representative or in probate, and a recipient of a Will gift of property takes it subject to debts. Also, no recipient of property who may lose it or who pays to keep it may have my estate or others pay or do exoneration.
    If during my life I disposed of an item in a specific gift then the gift is extinguished.
    I request and authorize any informal, summary, and quick probate or similar action. Any Personal Representative may act independently with no supervision of any court, including independent administration, and with no inventory, appraisal, or other action.
    I give any Personal Representative the a) fullest authority, discretion, and powers allowed by state law, b) power to lease, sell, mortgage, convey, or keep property including real property in a manner and time they deem helpful or proper, and c) authority to settle or pay claims or debts in the time and manner they choose. Any Personal Representative or other fiduciary shall have all powers and authorities conferred by statute or common law in any jurisdiction they may act, including powers and authorities conferred by Chapter 3B of the New Jersey Statutes Annotated including future amendments.

Any Guardian of any type, Conservator, Custodian, or other person managing a minor's property or money may use or invade the principal and sell property without court action.

If context permits the terms Personal Representative and Executor and Administrator are interchangeable, Conservator and Guardian of the Estate and Guardian of Property and Custodian are interchangeable, and residue and residuary are interchangeable. Any such person may stand in the place of and have all powers like the others named here.

The residue includes lapsed or failed gifts, insurance paid to the estate, digital assets, inheritances owed me, and all I had power of appointment or testamentary disposition over.

Any Personal Representative may access, manage, delete, modify, transfer, and otherwise control any digital accounts and assets I had any interest in or power over.

Any Personal Representative, Executor, Administrator, Guardian of any type like for a person or estate, Conservator, Custodian, and any other fiduciary under this Will or otherwise shall qualify and serve without bond, surety, security, surety bond, or similar.

If evidence does not show it likely a person survived me by 120 hours (5 days) then for this Will and my estate they shall be deemed in all ways as having died before me.

If part of this Will is by law invalid or unenforceable other provisions remain in effect.

Any Personal Representative may at any time transfer money or property of a minor under age 18 to a Custodian to serve under the New Jersey Uniform Transfers to Minors Act or similar law anywhere, and may pick a person to be Custodian including themselves.

TESTATOR

IN WITNESS WHEREOF, I declare that this instrument is my Will which I make as Testator and I have voluntarily signed on the ___ day of _____, 20___.

_____
Testator signature

WITNESSES

The foregoing instrument was signed by the Testator in our presence and declared by the Testator to be the Testator's Will, and we, the undersigned Witnesses, sign our names hereunto acting to witness the Will at the request and in the presence of the Testator, and in the presence of each other on the ___ day of _____, 20___.

_____   _____
Witness #1 signature   Witness #1 address

_____   _____
Witness #2 signature   Witness #2 address

CHAPTER 9
FORM 3: SELF-PROVING AFFIDAVIT

FORM CAN BE DONE TO MAKE USING A WILL LATER EASIER

This form is optional but can be done after a Will is done to help with legal work after a person's death. This form is a statutory form found written in New Jersey law for people to use.

FORM SAVES LATER WORK OF SHOWING WILL WAS PROPERLY SIGNED

A Self-Proving Affidavit "proves" a Will was signed properly. If this form is not done then after death a little work is need to get evidence from either witnesses to the Will signing, persons familiar with the signatures of people, or a handwriting expert. If this form is not done there is a bit more legal risk a Will won't be followed later. But of people doing Wills about <u>half skip a Self-Proving Affidavit</u> mostly due to hassle of finding a notary on top of 2 witnesses each time a Will is done or re-done, and since it mostly just saves a little later work of people who are happy to do work to get what the Will gives them.

FORM IS DONE BY TESTATOR AND 2 WITNESSES SIGNING BEFORE NOTARY

For this form to be valid a person who is a notary (also called a "notary public") must see the Testator and 2 witnesses sign and then the notary notarizes it. A notary can be found and politely asked to help at a bank, insurance agent, government office, or by looking in a phonebook. A notary is likelier to help if a person is an existing customer or pays. This form is often done a few minutes after a Will is signed but it can be done much later (even years later) when everyone can meet with a notary. This form can't legally be done before a Will is done. This form when done is often kept paper-clipped to the Will it supports.

SELF-PROVING AFFIDAVIT

(New Jersey Revised Statutes § 3B:3-5)

THE STATE OF NEW JERSEY

COUNTY OF _____

We _____, _____, and _____, the Testator and the Witnesses, respectively, whose names are signed to the attached or foregoing instrument, being duly sworn, do hereby declare to the undersigned authority that the Testator signed and executed the instrument as the Will of Testator and that the Testator had signed willingly, and that the Testator executed it as the Testator's free and voluntary act for the purposes therein expressed, and that each of the Witnesses, in the presence and hearing of the Testator, signed the Will acting to witness the Will and that to the best of the knowledge of each Witness the Testator was at that time 18 years of age or older, of sound mind and under no constraint or undue influence.

_____
Testator

_____   _____
Witness   Witness

Subscribed, sworn to and acknowledged before me by _____, the Testator, and subscribed and sworn to before me by _____ and _____, Witnesses, this ___ day of _____, 20___.

(SIGNED) _____
(Official capacity of officer) _____

CHAPTER 10
FORM 4: TANGIBLE PERSONAL PROPERTY MEMORANDUM

FORM LETS SOME GIFTS TO OCCUR AT DEATH BE ADDED OUTSIDE A WILL

This form lets people write to add some more gifts they want to occur after death. This form is often called by people a memo, list, or statement.

FORM GIVES EASY QUICK WAY TO WRITE MORE GIFTS OF PROPERTY

This form lets a person easily write some more gifts of property to occur at their death without having to re-write a Will. To use this form a valid Will must say that it can be used, and all this book's Will forms say this. If this form and a Will gift the same item then by law the Will controls. If more than 1 of these forms gift the same item then the more recently done page controls. People can modify an existing form page if they put a new date and signature on it. Note, to help avoid later delay this book's form says any of these forms not found within 90 days of a death will be ignored.

FORM CAN ONLY GIFT TANGIBLE PERSONAL PROPERTY

Under New Jersey law this form can only gift "tangible personal property". This means property that is <u>tangible</u> (touchable), so not accounts or moneys or investments related to papers, banks, or some entity like a corporation or partnership or trust. This also means property that is <u>personal property</u>, so not real property (land or buildings) and not fixtures (anything buried or tied to land). The form can't gift money whether coin or paper currency, even if it's an antique or foreign money. Most lawyers recommend people not use the form to give items used in a trade or business. Improper property written in the form is later just ignored. This form is often used to gift clothes, furniture, vehicles (including cars and trucks and boats), antiques, electronics, appliances, tools, building supplies, art, and jewelry.

It may help understanding to show the New Jersey law allowing this form, which in its main part says:

3B:3-11 Identifying devise of tangible personal property by separate writing.

A will may refer to a written statement or list to dispose of items of tangible personal property not otherwise specifically disposed of by the will, other than money.

[T]he writing must be either in the handwriting of the testator or be signed by the testator and must describe the items and the devisees with reasonable certainty.

The writing may be referred to as one to be in existence at the time of the testator's death; it may be prepared before or after the execution of the will; it may be altered by the testator after its preparation; and it may be a writing which has no significance apart from its effect on dispositions made by the will.

TO COMPLETE THE FORM A PERSON SIGNS AND DATES IT

This form to be legally valid just must be signed and usually dated by the person who is doing the form. Once completed this form is often kept with a Will. To cancel this form it can be destroyed, crossed out, or just thrown away so it is not found later.

TANGIBLE PERSONAL PROPERTY MEMORANDUM

In this writing are gifts of tangible personal property to occur at my death, but this writing if not found by someone within 90 days of my death is canceled.

I may do many pages of these writings which should all be seen as one document. If there are conflicts among such writings the provisions of the more recent writing will revoke the inconsistent provisions of a prior writing.

If a person getting a gift below does not survive me such gift is void and canceled.

DESCRIPTION OF PROPERTY		NAME OF PERSONS TO GET PROPERTY
_____	to	_____
_____	to	_____
_____	to	_____
_____	to	_____
_____	to	_____
_____	to	_____
_____	to	_____
_____	to	_____
_____	to	_____
_____	to	_____
_____	to	_____
_____	to	_____
_____	to	_____
_____	to	_____
_____	to	_____
_____	to	_____
_____	to	_____
_____	to	_____

Date:_____   Signed:_____

CHAPTER 11
FORM 5: HANDWRITTEN WILL

WILL CAN SKIP USING THE NORMAL 2 WITNESSES IF IT'S HANDWRITTEN

A Handwritten Will is a Will that is easier to do since it <u>does not need the usual 2 witnesses</u> if it is all handwritten by the person doing the Will.

HANDWRITTEN WILL WITHOUT WITNESSES IS ALLOWED IN NEW JERSEY

In 27 states including New Jersey a person doing a Will <u>can skip using the usual 2 witnesses</u> for a Will if: 1) it is all handwritten by the person doing the Will (not photocopied, typed, computer printed, or handwritten by anyone else), and 2) it is signed and dated. Many people call this a Handwritten Will but most lawyers call it a Holographic Will (Holo means Whole and Graph means Image in the Greek language). Politicians allow this since handwriting is harder to fake, people may be in an emergency or rush, witnesses may be scarce in the countryside, it is private, it can be cheap by skipping complexity and people, and it is traditional to do this especially in rural places. The 27 states that allow Handwritten Wills have about 55% of the U.S. population. See states with Handwritten Wills on map below <u>in dark</u>.

HANDWRITTEN WILLS ARE USUALLY FINE BUT REQUIRE LATER WORK

Some lawyers warn against Handwritten Wills saying they often read confusingly, skip legal words that help in some cases, and are found invalid more often – but some studies show they are liked and usually fine. To use a Handwritten Will later after a death some people must in writing or in testimony say the handwriting looks like the Testator's, which can be a hassle. But a normal Will if no Self-Proving Affidavit was done also needs similar proof like from a witness to the signing or other proof of signing. Handwritten Wills tend to be done by people who are young so unlikely to need a Will soon, who are in a hurry, who want to fix a mistake, who before a trip want to pick a Guardian, who moved to a new state, or who plan to do a better Will later.

WORDS BELOW ON THIS PAGE CAN BE USED FOR A HANDWRITTEN WILL

People can do a Handwritten Will in a sentence that is legal but may leave out helpful parts, for example: *"As my Will I give my estate and all else to Ann Baker who shall be Executor. - Dan Baker"* But it is recommended people use more complex words for a Handwritten Will shown on this page below. To do this people should change the names and words below on this page to match what they want done. If some people named to get things later die it is best to quickly re-do the Will and name different people. The last paragraph about Guardians for children can be skipped if a person has no children under age 18. This Will must be all handwritten by the person doing it on some paper (pencil is allowed) and then signed and dated by the person (usually in pen or permanent marker).

WILL

1. I am John Max Hill and I now live in Hudson County, New Jersey. I revoke any prior Wills and Codicils and declare this to be my Will.

2. I give my estate and all else to Jane Eve Hill and Wendy Sue Baker. My not giving to some other family of mine is intentional.

3. I name Jane Eve Hill as Personal Representative for me, my Will, and my estate. I request informal probate.

4. No bond or similar is needed for any Personal Representative or for any Guardian of any type.

5. If ever needed for a minor child I name Mary Ann Dodd as Guardian of the Person to have care, custody, and control of them.
I name this same person as Guardian of the Estate to have control and power over any minor child's property, money, and estate.

May 8, 2024   *John Max Hill*

CHAPTER 12
FORM 6: PROXY DIRECTIVE

FORM CAN NAME HEALTH CARE AGENT AND GIVE INSTRUCTIONS

This form lets a person, just in case it is later needed, name someone to control health care and write health care instructions. This form is usually too long for paramedics and similar people to read and follow. This book's form is written by a state health care commission and is on the state Department of Health webpage. *See htttps://www.nj.gov/health/advancedirective/ad/forums-faqs*. Most people do this 1 form and skip other health care forms. This form is often called a "Durable Power Of Attorney For Health Care".

PERSON CAN NAME AN AGENT TO HAVE POWER OVER HEALTH CARE

This form lets someone be named as "Proxy" to have power to make medical decisions for the person who did the form. Sometimes this person is called the "Health Care Agent". Usually the Proxy only acts when the sick person is incapacitated and can't control their own health care. A person with capacity and still thinking well can over-rule their Proxy or fire them. Doing this form to name family like a spouse or a friend as Proxy can avoid them having to rush to see a judge to have more power in a medical emergency. The Proxy should do what the sick person requested or likely would want done.

FORM CAN GIVE HEALTH CARE INSTRUCTIONS

In the form a person can give written health care instructions that family, Proxy, and doctors must all legally follow. But many people skip written instructions since they are hard to write to cover all medical situations and if instructions are not clear they can cause legal problems. In the form a person can name a Proxy but skip instructions, or can do instructions and skip naming a Proxy.

FORM IS SIGNED WITH 2 WITNESSES

The form is completed by a person signing with 2 witnesses who then also sign. A witness should be a person at least age 18, not the Proxy (Agent) with power over health care, not a doctor or nurse or similar person involved in a person's care, and usually not a person who may inherit or benefit much from a death. Often used as witnesses are family, friends, or strangers. Once done the form usually is shown to places that may give care to be made a part of a person's medical file and followed. Some people keep a copy of the form handy to show if needed. To cancel the form a person should tell their Proxy and also usually tell any places that saw the form that it is canceled.

The New Jersey Commission on Legal and Ethical Problems in the Delivery of Health Care

PROXY DIRECTIVE--(Durable Power of Attorney for Health Care)
Designation of Health Care Representative

I understand that as a competent adult, I have the right to make decisions about my health care. There may come a time when I am unable, due to physical or mental incapacity, to make my own health care decision. In these circumstances, those caring for me will need direction and they will turn to someone who knows my values and health care wishes. By writing this durable power of attorney for health care I appoint a health care representative with the legal authority to make health care decisions on my behalf and to consult with my physician and others. I direct that this document become part of my permanent medical records.

A) CHOOSING A HEALTH CARE REPRESENTATIVE:

I, _____, hereby designate _____,
of _____
_____,
(home address and telephone number of health care representative)

as my health care representative to make any and all health care decisions for me, including decisions to accept or to refuse any treatment, service or procedure used to diagnose or treat my physical or mental condition and decisions to provide, withhold or withdraw life-sustaining measures. I direct my representative to make decisions on my behalf in accordance with my wishes as stated in this document, or as otherwise known to him or her. In the event my wishes are not clear, my representative is authorized to make decisions in my best interest, based on what is known of my wishes.

This durable power of attorney for health care shall take effect in the event I become unable to make my own health care decisions, as determined by the physician who has primary responsibility for my care, and any necessary confirming determinations.

B) ALTERNATE REPRESENTATIVES:
If the person I have designated above is unable, unwilling or unavailable to act as my health care representative, I hereby designate the following person(s) to act as my health care representative, in the order of priority stated:

1. *name* _____
   address _____
   city _____ *state* _____
   telephone _____

2. *name* _____
   address _____
   city _____ *state* _____
   telephone _____

C) SPECIFIC DIRECTIONS: Please initial the statement below which best expresses your wishes.

_____ My health care representative is authorized to direct that artificially provided fluids and nutrition, such as by feeding tube or intravenous infusion, be withheld or withdrawn.

_____ My health care representative does not have this authority, and I direct that artificially provided fluids and nutrition be provided to preserve my life, to the extent medically appropriate.

The New Jersey Commission on Legal and Ethical Problems in the Delivery of Health Care

(If you have any additional specific instructions concerning your care you may use the space below or attach an additional statement.)

_____
_____
_____
_____

D) COPIES: The original or a copy of this document has been given to my health care representative and to the following:

1. name _____
   address _____
   city _____ state _____ telephone _____

2. name _____
   address _____
   city _____ state _____ telephone _____

E) SIGNATURE: By writing this durable power of attorney for health care, I inform those who may become entrusted with my care of my health care wishes and intend to ease the burdens of decision making which this responsibility may impose. I have discussed the terms of this designation with my health care representative and he or she has willingly agreed to accept the responsibility for acting on my behalf in accordance with my wishes as expressed in this document. I understand the purpose and effect of this document and sign it knowingly, voluntarily and after careful deliberation.

Signed this _____ **day of** _____, 20_____.

signature _____
address _____
city _____ state _____

F) WITNESSES: I declare that the person who signed this document, or asked another to sign this document on his or her behalf, did so in my presence, that he or she is personally known to me, and that he or she appears to be of sound mind and free of duress or undue influence. I am 18 years of age or older, and am not designated by this or any other document as the person's health care representative, nor as an alternate health care representative.

1. witness _____ 2. witness _____
   address _____   address _____
   city _____ state _____   city _____ state _____
   signature _____   signature _____
   date _____   date _____

CHAPTER 13
FORM 7: INSTRUCTION DIRECTIVE

IN FORM CAN SAY STOP CARE IF DOCTORS LATER THINK IT WON'T HELP

This form lets a person do the serious act of saying to stop certain health care if <u>later</u> the doctors think more medical care won't help. This form is usually too long for paramedics and others in a hurry to read. This form was written by an official state commission and is on the state Department of Health webpage. See *https://www.nj.gov/health/advancedirective/ad/forums-faqs*. This form is often called a "Living Will".

IN FORM CAN SAY STOP HEALTH CARE IF IT WON'T HELP

In the form a person can say to stop health care if <u>later</u> doctors think a person is <u>incapacitated</u> (so can't make decisions about their own care), has <u>very bad health</u>, and <u>more medical care won't help</u>. Many people also use the form to give specific instructions like on a) cardio-pulmonary resuscitation (CPR) or electric shocks to restart the heart or breathing, and b) giving food or water by tube or similar less natural means. The care being stopped is often called "life-sustaining". Pain relief and comfort care usually does continue. Doctors can help people fill out and use this form.

SIGN FORM WITH 2 WITNESSES WHO ALSO SIGN

The form is completed by a person signing with 2 witnesses who also sign. A person to be a witness should be at least age 18, not named a Proxy (Agent) with power over health care, not be a doctor or nurse or similar person involved in a person's health care, and not be a person who may inherit or financially benefit from a death. Witnesses can be other family, friends, co-workers, or strangers. Once done a person usually shows the form to any place that may give care to make it part of a person's medical file and followed. Some people keep the form nearby to show people if needed.

The New Jersey Commission on Legal and Ethical Problems in the Delivery of Health Care

INSTRUCTION DIRECTIVE

I understand that as a competent adult I have the right to make decisions about my health care. There may come a time when I am unable, due to physical or mental incapacity, to make my own health care decisions. In these circumstances, those caring for me will need direction concerning my care and they will require information about my values and health care wishes. In order to provide the guidance and authority needed to make decisions on my behalf:

A) I, _____, hereby declare and make known to my family, physician, and others, my instructions and wishes for my future health care. I direct that all health care decisions, including decisions to accept or refuse any treatment, service or procedure used to diagnose, treat or care for my physical or mental condition and decisions to provide, withhold or withdraw life-sustaining measures, be made in accordance with my wishes as expressed in this document. This instruction directive shall take effect in the event I become unable to make my own health care decisions, as determined by the physician who has primary responsibility for my care, and any necessary confirming determinations. I direct that this document become part of my permanent medical records.

Part One: Statement of My Wishes Concerning My Future Health Care

*In **Part One**, you are asked to provide instructions concerning your future health care. This will require making important and perhaps difficult choices. Before completing your directive, you should discuss these matters with your doctor, family members or others who may become responsible for your care.*

*In **Section B and C**, you may state the circumstances in which various forms of medical treatment, including life-sustaining measures, should be provided, withheld or discontinued. If the options and choices below do not fully express your wishes, you should use **Section D**, and/or attach a statement to this document which would provide those responsible for your care with additional information you think would help them in making decisions about your medical treatment.* **Please familiarize yourself with all sections of Part One before completing your directive.**

B) **GENERAL INSTRUCTIONS:** To inform those responsible for my care of my specific wishes, I make the following statement of personal views regarding my health care:

Initial ONE of the following two statements with which you agree:

1. _____ I direct that all medically appropriate measures be provided to sustain my life, regardless of my physical or mental condition

2. _____ There are circumstances in which I would not want my life to be prolonged by further medical treatment. In these circumstances, life-sustaining measures should not be initiated and if they have been, they should be discontinued. I recognize that this is likely to hasten my death. In the following, I specify the circumstances in which I would choose to forego life-sustaining measures.

The New Jersey Commission on Legal and Ethical Problems in the Delivery of Health Care

If you have initialed statement 2 on page 1, please initial each of the statements (a, b, c) with which you agree:

a. _____ I realize that there may come a time when I am diagnosed as having an incurable and irreversible illness, disease, or condition. If this occurs, and my attending physician and at least one additional physician who has personally examined me determine that my condition is **terminal**, I direct that life-sustaining measures which would serve only to artificially prolong my dying be withheld or discontinued. I also direct that I be given all medically appropriate care necessary to make me comfortable and to relieve pain.

In the space provided, write in the bracketed phrase with which you agree:

To me, terminal condition means that my physicians have determined that:

_____

[I will die within a few days]   [I will die within a few weeks]
[I have a life expectancy of approximately _____ or less *(enter 6 months, or 1 year)***]**

b. _____ If there should come a time when I come **permanently unconscious**, and it is determined by my attending physician and at least one additional physician with appropriate expertise who has personally examined me, that I have totally and irreversibly lost consciousness and my capacity for interaction with other people and my surroundings, I direct that life-sustaining measures be withheld or discontinued. I understand that I will not experience pain or discomfort in this condition, and I direct that I be given all my medically appropriate care necessary to provide for my personal hygiene and dignity.

c. _____ I realize that there may come a time when I am diagnosed as having an **incurable and irreversible** illness, disease, or condition which may not be terminal. My condition may cause me to experience severe and progressive physical or mental deterioration and/or a permanent loss of capacities and faculties I value highly. If, in the course of my medical care, the burdens of continued life with treatment become greater than the benefits I experience, I direct that life-sustaining measures be withheld or discontinued. I also direct that I be given all medically appropriate care necessary to make me comfortable and to relieve pain.

*(Paragraph c. covers a wide range of possible situations in which you may have experienced partial or complete loss of certain mental and physical capacities you value highly. If you wish, in the space provided below you may specify in more detail the conditions in which you would choose to forego life-sustaining measures. You might include a description of the faculties or capacities, which, if irretrievably lost would lead you to accept death rather than continue living. You may want to express any special concerns you have about particular medical conditions or treatments, or any other considerations which would provide further guidance to those who may become responsible for your care. If necessary, you may attach a separate statement to this document or use **Section D** to provide additional instructions.)*

Examples of conditions which I find unacceptable are:

_____
_____
_____
_____

The New Jersey Commission on Legal and Ethical Problems in the Delivery of Health Care

C) SPECIFIC INSTRUCTIONS: Artificially Provided Fluids and Nutrition; Cardiopulmonary Resuscitation (CPR). *On page 2 you provided general instructions regarding life-sustaining measures. Here you are asked to give specific instructions regarding two types of life-sustaining measures-artificially provided fluids and nutrition and cardiopulmonary resuscitation.*

In the space provided, write in the bracketed phrase with which you agree:

1. In the circumstances I initialed on page 2, I also direct that artificially provided fluids and nutrition, such as by feeding tube or intravenous infusion,

    _____

    [be withheld or withdrawn and that I be allowed to die]
    [be provided to the extent medically appropriate]

2. In the circumstances I initialed on page 2, if I should suffer a cardiac arrest, I also direct that cardiopulmonary resuscitation (CPR)

    _____

    [not be provided and that I be allowed to die]
    [be provided to preserve my life, unless medically inappropriate or futile]

3. If neither of the above statements adequately expresses your wishes concerning artificially provided fluids and nutrition or CPR, please explain your wishes below.

    _____
    _____
    _____

D) ADDITIONAL INSTRUCTIONS: *(You should provide any additional information about your health care preferences which is important to you and which may help those concerned with your care to implement your wishes. You may wish to direct your family members or your health care providers to consult with others, or you may wish to direct that your care be provided by a particular physician, hospital, nursing home, or at home. If you are or believe you may become pregnant, you may wish to state specific instructions. If you need more space than is provided here you may attach an additional statement to this directive.)*

_____
_____
_____

E) BRAIN DEATH: *(The State of New Jersey recognizes the irreversible cessation of all functions of the entire brain, including the brain stem (also known as whole brain death), as a legal standard for the declaration of death. However, individuals who cannot accept this standard because of their personal religious beliefs may request that it not be applied in determining their death.)*

Initial the following statement only if it applies to you:

_____ To declare my death on the basis of the whole brain death standard would violate my personal religious beliefs. I therefore wish my death to be declared solely on the basis of the traditional criteria of irreversible cessation of cardiopulmonary (heartbeat and breathing) function.

The New Jersey Commission on Legal and Ethical Problems in the Delivery of Health Care

---

F) AFTER DEATH - ANATOMICAL GIFTS: *(It is now possible to transplant human organs and tissue in order to save and improve the lives of others. Organs, tissues and other body parts are also used for therapy, medical research and education. This section allows you to indicate your desire to make an anatomical gift and if so, to provide instructions for any limitations or special uses.)*

Initial the statements which express your wishes:

1. _____ **I wish** to make the following anatomical gift to take effect upon my death:

   A. _____ any needed organs or body parts
   B. _____ only the following organs or parts

   _____

for the purposes of transplantation, therapy, medical research or education, or

   C. _____ my body for anatomical study, if needed.
   D. _____ special limitations, if any:

   _____

If you wish to provide additional instructions, such as indicating your preference that your organs be given to a specific person or institution, or be used for a specific purpose, please do so in the space provided below.

_____
_____
_____

2. _____ **I do not wish** to make an anatomical gift upon my death.

Part Two: Signature and Witnesses

G) COPIES: The original or a copy of this document has been given to the following people *(NOTE: It is important that you provide a family member, friend or your physician with a copy of your directive.)*:

1. name _____   2. name _____

   address _____   address _____

   city _____ state _____   city _____ state _____

   telephone _____   telephone _____

The New Jersey Commission on Legal and Ethical Problems in the Delivery of Health Care

H) SIGNATURE: By writing this advance directive, I inform those who may become entrusted with my health care of my wishes and intend to ease the burdens of decision making which this responsibility may impose. I understand the purpose and effect of this document and sign it knowingly, voluntarily and after careful deliberation.

Signed this _____ **day of** _____, **20**_____.

signature _____

address _____

city _____ *state* _____

I) WITNESSES: I declare that the person who signed this document, or asked another to sign this document on his or her behalf, did so in my presence, that he or she is personally known to me and that he or she appears to be of sound mind and free of duress or undue influence. I am 18 years of age or older, and am not designated by this or any other document as the person's health care representative nor as an alternate health care representative.

1. *witness* _____

   address _____

   city _____ *state* _____

   signature _____

   date _____

2. *witness* _____

   address _____

   city _____ *state* _____

   signature _____

   date _____

CHAPTER 14
FORM 8: PRACTITIONER ORDERS FOR LIFE-SUSTAINING TREATMENT

FORM SAYS TO IMMEDIATELY NO LONGER TRY HEALTH CARE

The Practitioner Orders for Life-Sustaining Treatment form, which is often called the "P.O.L.S.T." form, says to immediately no longer try certain medical care. Doing this is very serious and rare. The form is short so it can be read fast and quickly followed (like by paramedics) and it can be used outside a health facility, but it can be used in places too. This book's form is a standard form. Most other states have a similar form.

IN FORM CAN SAY TO IMMEDIATELY NO LONGER TRY CERTAIN HEALTH CARE

In the form a person can say to immediately no longer try certain health care. The form has different sections which are described below. If a person doing the form skips a section that mostly means all care and actions covered by the section should be done.

■ Section A is a place where the patient can write health goals, but this section doesn't legally do much so is often skipped by people.

■ Section B covers the level of treatment intervention wanted, like saying not to transfer person to hospital.

■ Section C is on giving fluids or nutrition by tube or similar ways (when a person can't drink or eat normally).

■ Section D is on C.P.R. ("cardio-pulmonary resuscitation") to restart the heart or breathing and this includes electric shocks (defibrillation) and, also, is about breathing by tube. **This section is the most used section**.

■ Section E says if a person is incapacitated but named someone here to act for them, then that person can modify this P.O.L.S.T. form. Many people skip this section to not name anyone here.

Note, instead of the P.O.L.S.T. form a few people use the "Do-Not-Resuscitate" form by the Medical Society of New Jersey, but this other form only covers C.P.R. and is less often used. In practice far more people use the P.O.L.S.T. form but then a bit mistakenly they call it the Do-Not-Resuscitate form.

PERSON AND A DOCTOR MUST SIGN THE FORM

The form must be signed by the person doing form and their doctor or similar person (called in the form the "practitioner"). Doctors can explain form options and give form copies (often on green paper to be easily spotted by paramedics). Once completed this form is usually shown to places that may give care to make it part of medical files to follow. A person might keep a copy handy to show if needed like to paramedics and similar people who may try to give care (a special bracelet or necklace from a doctor also may be worn). To cancel the form a person (unless they lack mental capacity) should clearly tell places that may give care and are aware of the form that it's now canceled.

HIPAA PERMITS DISCLOSURE OF POLST TO OTHER HEALTHCARE PROFESSIONALS AS NECESSARY

NEW JERSEY PRACTITIONER ORDERS FOR LIFE-SUSTAINING TREATMENT (POLST)

Follow these orders, then contact physician/APN/PA. This Medical Order Sheet is based on the current medical condition of the person referenced below and their wishes stated verbally or in a written advance directive. Any section not completed implies full treatment for that section. Everyone will be treated with dignity and respect.

Person's Name (last, first, middle) | Date of Birth

Print Person's Address

A — GOALS OF CARE
(See reverse for instructions. This section does not constitute a medical order.)

B — MEDICAL INTERVENTIONS *Person is breathing and/or has a pulse*

❏ **Full Treatment.** Use all appropriate medical and surgical interventions as indicated to support life. If in a nursing facility, transfer to hospital if indicated. See section D for resuscitation status.

❏ **Limited Treatment.** Use appropriate medical treatment such as antibiotics and IV fluids as indicated. May use non-invasive positive airway pressure. Generally avoid intensive care.
 ❏ Transfer to hospital for medical interventions. ❏ Transfer to hospital only if comfort needs cannot be met in current location.

❏ **Symptom Treatment Only.** Use aggressive comfort treatment to relieve pain and suffering by using any medication by any route, positioning, wound care and other measures. Use oxygen, suctioning and manual treatment of airway obstruction as needed for comfort. Use antibiotics only to promote comfort. Transfer only if comfort needs cannot be met in current location.

Additional Orders: _____

C — ARTIFICIALLY ADMINISTERED FLUIDS AND NUTRITION *Always offer food/fluids by mouth, if feasible and desired*

❏ No artificial nutrition   ❏ Long-term artificial nutrition   ❏ Defined trial period of artificial nutrition

D

CARDIOPULMONARY RESUSCITATION (CPR)
Person has no pulse and/or is not breathing
❏ Attempt resuscitation/CPR
❏ Do not attempt resuscitation/DNAR
  Allow Natural Death

AIRWAY MANAGEMENT *Person is in respiratory distress with a pulse*
❏ Intubate/use artificial ventilation as needed
❏ Do not intubate - Use O2, manual treatment to relieve airway obstruction, medications for comfort
❏ Additional Order (for example defined trial period of mechanical ventilation)
_____
_____

E
If I lose my decision-making capacity, I authorize my surrogate decision-maker, listed below, to modify or revoke the NJ POLST orders in consultation with my treating physician/APN/PA in keeping with my goals: ❏ Yes ❏ No

F — SIGNATURES
I have discussed this information with my physician/APN/PA

Print Name _____

Signature _____

❏ Person Named Above   ❏ Spouse/Civil Union Partner
❏ Health Care Representative/   ❏ Parent of Minor
  Legal Guardian   ❏ Other Surrogate

Has the person named above made an anatomical gift:
❏ Yes ❏ No ❏ Unknown

These orders are consistent with the person's medical condition, known preferences and best known information.

PRINT - Physician/APN/PA Name | Phone Number

Physician/APN/PA Signature (Mandatory) | Date/Time

Professional License Number

SURROGATE INFORMATION
Surrogate listed here is the healthcare representative previously identified in an advance directive: ❏ Yes ❏ No ❏ Unknown

Print Name of Surrogate | Phone Number

Print Surrogate Address

■ Surrogate listed is only authorized to change this form if "yes" is checked in Section E above.

August 2019   **SEND ORIGINAL FORM WITH PERSON, WHENEVER TRANSFERRED**

HIPAA PERMITS DISCLOSURE OF POLST TO OTHER HEALTHCARE PROFESSIONALS AS NECESSARY

DIRECTIONS FOR HEALTHCARE PROFESSIONAL

COMPLETING POLST
- Must be completed by a physician, advance practice nurse or physician assistant.
- Use of original form is strongly encouraged. Photocopies and faxes of signed POLST forms may be used.
- Any incomplete section of POLST implies full treatment for that section.

REVIEWING POLST
POLST orders are actual orders that transfer with the person and are valid in all settings in New Jersey. It is recommended that POLST be reviewed periodically, especially when:
- The person is transferred from one care setting or care level to another, or
- There is a substantial change in the person's health status, or
- The person's treatment preferences change.

MODIFYING AND VOIDING POLST – *An individual with decision-making capacity can always modify/void a POLST at any time.*
- A surrogate, if authorized in Section E on the front of this form, may, at any time, void the POLST form, change his/her mind about the treatment preferences or execute a new POLST document based upon the person's known wishes or other documentation such as an advance directive.
- A surrogate decision-maker, if authorized on this form to do so, may request to modify the orders based on the known desires of the person or, if unknown, the person's best interests.
- To void POLST, draw a line through all sections and write "VOID" in large letters. Sign and date this line.

Section A
What are the specific goals that we are trying to achieve by this treatment plan of care? This can be determined by asking the simple question: "What are your hopes for the future?" Examples include but are not restricted to:
- Longevity, cure, remission
- Better quality of life
- Live long enough to attend a family event (wedding, birthday, graduation)
- Live without pain, nausea, shortness of breath
- Activities such as eating, driving, gardening, enjoying grandchildren

Medical providers are encouraged to share information regarding prognosis to enable the person to set realistic goals.

Section B
- When "limited treatment" is selected, also indicate if the person prefers or does not prefer to be transferred to a hospital for additional care.
- IV medication to enhance comfort may be appropriate for a person who has chosen "symptom treatment only."
- Non-invasive positive airway pressure includes continuous positive airway pressure (CPAP) or bi-level positive airway pressure (BiPAP).
- Comfort measures will always be provided.

Section C
Oral fluids and nutrition should always be offered if medically feasible and if they meet the goals of care determined by the person or surrogate. The administration of nutrition and hydration whether orally or by invasive means shall be within the context of the person's wishes, religion and cultural beliefs.

Section D
Make a selection for the person's preferences regarding CPR and a separate selection regarding airway management. A defined trial period of mechanical ventilation may be considered, for example, when additional time is needed to assess the current clinical situation or when the expected need would be short term and may provide some palliative benefit.

Section E
This section is applicable in situations where the person has decision-making capacity when the POLST form is completed. A surrogate may only void or modify an existing POLST form, or execute a new one, if authorized in this section by the person.

Section F
POLST must be signed by a practitioner, meaning a physician, APN or PA, to be valid. Verbal orders are acceptable with follow-up signature by the physician/APN/PA in accordance with facility/community policy. POLST orders should be signed by the person/surrogate. Indicate on the signature line if the person/surrogate is unable to sign, declined to sign, or a verbal consent is given. Remind the person/surrogate that once completed and signed, this POLST will void any prior POLST documents.

SEND ORIGINAL FORM WITH PERSON, WHENEVER TRANSFERRED

CHAPTER 15
FORM 9: DURABLE GENERAL POWER OF ATTORNEY

FORM LETS PERSON GIVE POWER OVER THEIR PROPERTY AND MONEY

This form lets a person give power to someone to let them do things with the person's money, property, debt, and other things. Many people call this a "Financial Power of Attorney".

FORM GIVES POWER TO LET SOMEONE CONTROL PROPERTY AND MONEY

The form lets a person (called in the form the "Principal") give power to someone (who is called in the form the "Agent" or "Attorney-in-Fact") to do things to control the person's money, property, and other things. Doing this can let the Agent help use accounts, pay bills, buy or sell things, sign contracts, take out debt, hire workers, and get information from banks and others. Often named as Agent is a trusted person like a spouse, other relative, or a close friend. Doing this form might avoid need for a nursing home, guardian, conservator, or other serious actions. Note, a person until they are incapacitated can act for themselves or overrule their Agent and even fire the Agent. This form is often called "General" since power given is not narrow, and called "Durable" since power of the form continues even after a person is incapacitated.

DUE TO RISKS MANY SKIP THIS FORM OR CONSULT A LAWYER

Many people skip this form or first see a lawyer. Using this form is risky and can lead to harm since the Agent can be wasteful with money, commit fraud or theft, or by carelessness allow some other harms. A person acting as Agent has a duty to be loyal and act reasonably and can be sued for any harm, but they may later be out of money to pay. Usually banks and others can't be blamed for obeying an Agent's orders. The law is complex and basic acts of an Agent may be fine like paying bills, but some acts may be improper like making gifts, risky investments, or unusual acts. It is best a person not the Agent does anything unusual.

PERSON SHOULD SIGN FORM WITH A NOTARY AND USUALLY 2 WITNESSES

This form legally just needs to be signed by a person with a notary present who then notarizes it, but it is common to also have 2 persons act as witnesses who then also sign. Witnesses should be at least age 18, not named Agent in the form, and not be close family if possible. At the end is a spot for the person getting power to accept their position but this can be done later. The completed form can be kept by a person till needed but often the form is quickly given to the Agent getting power to hold and use if needed. To cancel the form a person usually tells the Agent it is canceled and takes back any copies, and then maybe tells all places that saw the form that it is canceled.

DURABLE GENERAL POWER OF ATTORNEY

NOTICE: POWERS GRANTED BY THIS ARE BROAD AND SWEEPING. IF YOU HAVE QUESTIONS ABOUT THIS DOCUMENT SEEK LEGAL ADVICE. THIS DOCUMENT DOES NOT LET ANYONE TO MAKE HEALTH CARE DECISIONS FOR YOU. YOU MAY REVOKE THIS DOCUMENT AT ANY TIME.

I, _____ , who lives at _____
_____, do now create a Durable General Power of Attorney under New Jersey law.

I appoint _____ to serve as my Attorney-in-Fact.

I immediately give my Attorney-in-Fact total and full power and authority to act for me in any way including in any way I myself could do if I were personally present. This document is and should be interpreted as a durable general power of attorney. My Attorney-in-Fact may do everything necessary or convenient to exercise their power and authority.

This Durable General Power of Attorney and authority granted to my Attorney-in-Fact are granted and effective immediately upon signing.

This Power of Attorney shall not be affected by subsequent disability or incapacity of the principal, or by lapse of time.

My Attorney-in-Fact is specifically empowered to conduct banking transactions as set forth in Section 2 of P.L. 1991, c.95 (C.46:2B-11), as provided by New Jersey law.

My Attorney-in-Fact is specifically authorized and given power to access and add or remove property from a safe-deposit box in my name or which I am an authorized signer, including a box involving others.

My Attorney-in-Fact is specifically authorized and given power to sign, execute, endorse, seal, acknowledge, deliver, and file or record all legal and other documents.

I agree a third party who receives a copy of this document may immediately act upon it. Revocation is not effective as to a third party until they actually learn of the revocation. I agree to indemnify the third party for any claims that arise against the third party because of reliance on this document.

Notwithstanding any other provision no power or authority over health care is given.

SIGNATURE OF PRINCIPAL

_____   _____
Signature of Principal   Date

NOTARY

STATE OF NEW JERSEY   )
COUNTY OF _____) ss.

Sworn before me this ___ day of _____, 20___, there personally appeared _____, as Principal, personally known to me (or proved to me on the basis of satisfactory evidence) to be the individual whose name is subscribed to the foregoing Durable General Power of Attorney, and he or she acknowledged he or she executed the same as their voluntary act and deed for the purposes therein contained.

Signature of Notary _____

WITNESSES

The foregoing Durable General Power of Attorney was, on date written above, published and declared by Principal, in our presence to be his Durable General Power of Attorney. We, at Principal's request and in his or her presence, and the presence of each other, have attested to the same and signed as attesting witnesses. We declare that at time of our attestation of this instrument that each of us was at least age 18 and of sound mind and that Principal was, to the best of our knowledge and belief, of sound mind and memory and under no undue duress or constraint.

_____   _____
Signature of Witness   Signature of Witness

ATTORNEY-IN-FACT ACCEPTANCE

The undersigned Attorney-in-Fact hereby accepts the power and authority set out in this Durable General Power of Attorney and the associated duties and responsibilities.

_____   _____
Signature of Attorney-in-Fact   Date

CHAPTER 16
FORM 10: POWER OF ATTORNEY AND DELEGATION OF AUTHORITY BY PARENT CONCERNING MINOR CHILD

FORM LETS PARENT GIVE POWER TO SOMEONE OVER A MINOR CHILD

This form lets a parent give power over a minor child under age 18 to someone they name to let them make decisions about the child. New Jersey law has a statutory form at New Jersey Statutes § 3B:12-39, and this book's form is based on this statutory form with small changes.

FORM GIVES POWER OVER CHILD TO SOMEONE

This form lets a parent give power over a child under 18 to someone to <u>let them help make decisions if needed</u>. Often named is a family member, friend, or a teacher or coach. The form calls itself a "Power of Attorney" form, the person giving power the "Principal", and the person getting power the "Attorney-in-Fact" and also "Alternative Caregiver". <u>The parent who gave power can always over-rule the person or fire them</u>. The form can help in many situations when a parent and child are apart, like for school, travel, family visit, work, prison, rehab, sports, or medical care (like if a parent can't always be at a hospital a child is staying in). This form is mostly not used for brief periods. Some people do use the form to give power to a relative if they are helping with a child most days. By law the form gives no power to agree to marriage or adoption. New Jersey law <u>limits this form to lasting 1 year</u> but after this people are free to re-do the form.

FORM HAS MANY PARTS TO FILL IN

The form has many parts for a parent to do.

<u>First</u> is a place to put names of 1 or 2 parents doing the form and the person getting power.
<u>Second</u> is a place to explain if the 2nd parent is not signing why not, but if they do sign this can be skipped.
<u>Third</u> is a place to put the name and birth date of child – and people with many children can do many copies.
<u>Fourth</u> is place to pick powers to give by check mark. Often most powers are given especially health care.
<u>Fifth</u> is a place to say when the form has power and <u>most people pick the option to say it starts when signed</u>.
<u>Sixth</u> is a place that comes before the signature area and it has some very standard legal language.
<u>Next to last</u> is a place for 1 or 2 parents to sign and for 2 witnesses to sign and put the witness's addresses.
<u>Finally</u> is an optional place for a notary which has a separate notary area for each parent who is signing.

PERSON MUST SIGN FORM WITH 2 WITNESSES AND USUALLY A NOTARY

This form must be signed by 1 or 2 parents in front of 2 witnesses who then also sign. Anyone at least 18 can be a witness except the person getting power in the form. There is also an area for a notary to also sign and notarize for each parent who is signing, and this notary is optional but common and it makes the form more likely to be followed. Once completed a parent can keep the form until needed or hand it out to the person getting power. Note, instead of a parent a "guardian" or "custodian" of a child can also use this form by replacing the term "parent" with these other terms.

POWER OF ATTORNEY AND DELEGATION OF AUTHORITY BY PARENT CONCERNING MINOR CHILD
PURSUANT TO N.J.S. 3B : 12-39

(Note: This form is slightly modified from the statutory form found at New Jersey Statutes 3B :12-39.)

1. **This power of attorney is made between the following** _____
(name(s), of parent(s)) residing at _____
_____(address(es) and reachable at
_____(telephone number(s), referred to as the Principal(s)

and _____(name of alternative caregiver),
referred to here as attorney-in-fact, residing at _____
_____ (home address of alternative caregiver) and
reachable at _____(telephone number of alternative caregiver).

2. If a parent is signing, the other parent must generally also sign below to show consent. Similarly, if a custodian who shares legal custody with a parent is signing, the parent who shares legal custody must generally also sign below to show consent. **If such other parent does not sign below, please check off reason(s) to explain why**:

_____ Such parent is deceased.

_____ By order of a court of competent jurisdiction, such parent retains neither legal nor physical custody of child(ren).

_____ Such parent is mentally or physically unable to give consent.

_____ Such parent has not been involved in raising or financially supporting child(ren) for two years or a third of the life of the child(ren), whichever is less, immediately preceding the date of the latest signature below.

_____ Identity or whereabouts of such parent are unknown to me.

_____ Despite diligent efforts described below, I was unable to reach such parent.

Diligent efforts included:_____
_____
_____

Other:_____
_____
_____

3. This power of attorney concerns and gives power **over my/our child who is known as** _____ , (name of minor child) , born on _____ day of _____ , 20____ .

4. I/we appoint said attorney-in-fact, pursuant to N.J.S.3B:12-39 , and delegate to said attorney-in-fact **the following powers**, all of which I/we possess, concerning the care, custody, and/or property of my/our minor child, **(check all that apply):**

_____ **Care-Giving.** The attorney-in-fact shall have temporary care-giving authority for the minor child(ren)), until such time as the minor child(ren) is/are returned to my/our physical custody, or his/her/their custody status is altered by a federal, state, or local agency; or changed by a court of law.

_____ **Well-Being.** The attorney-in-fact shall have power to provide for the physical and mental well-being of the minor child(ren)), including, but not limited to, providing food and shelter.

_____ **Education.** The attorney-in-fact shall have the authority to enroll the minor child(ren) in the appropriate educational institutions; obtain access to his/her/their school records; authorize his/her/their participation in school activities; and make any and all decisions related to his/her/their education, including, but not limited to, those related to special education.

_____ **Health Care.** The attorney-in-fact shall have the authority, to the same extent that a parent/custodian/guardian would have the authority, to make medical, dental, and mental health decisions; to sign documents, waivers, and releases required by a hospital or physician; to access medical, dental, or mental health records concerning the minor child(ren); to authorize the minor child(ren)' admission to or discharge from any hospital or medical care facility; to consult with any health care provider; to consent to the provision, withholding, modification, or withdrawal of any health care procedure; and to make other decisions related to the health care needs of the minor child(ren).

_____ **Travel.** The attorney-in-fact shall have the authority to make travel arrangements on behalf of the minor child(ren) for destinations both inside and outside of the United States by air and/or ground transportation; to accompany the minor child(ren) on any such trips; and to make any and all related arrangements on behalf of the minor child(ren)), including, but not limited to, hotel accommodations.

_____ **Financial Interests.** The attorney-in-fact may handle any and all financial affairs and any and all personal and legal matters concerning the minor child(ren).

_____ **All Other Powers.** The attorney-in-fact shall have the authority to handle and engage in any and all other matters relating to the care, custody, and property of the minor child(ren) which are permitted pursuant to applicable State law.

_____ **Other specific authority:**_____
_____
_____

5. By this delegation, I/we provide that the attorney-in-fact's **authority shall take effect upon the following "activating event(s)", (check all that apply):**

_____ The execution of this document on the latest date below; or

_____ My attending physician concludes that I am incapacitated, and thus unable to care for my minor child(ren); or

_____ My attending physician concludes that I am physically debilitated, and thus unable to care for my minor child(ren); or

_____ I am detained in immigration detention, removed, or deported; or

_____ I am incarcerated based on criminal charges, including pending charges, or conviction; or

_____ I am deployed in military service; or

_____ Upon my death, if I have made no more permanent care arrangements for my minor child; or

_____ Other (specify reason):_____
_____
_____.

6. I/we understand that **this delegation will expire one year from the execution of this document** on the latest date below, and that the authority of the attorney-in-fact, if any, will cease, **unless** by that date (i) I renew this delegation, by the same process applicable to the original delegation; (ii) a court of competent jurisdiction appoints a custodian, guardian, or standby guardian for the minor child(ren); or (iii) exigent circumstances make it impossible for me to renew this delegation, and I have not made alternative care arrangements for my minor child(ren).

I/we hereby authorize that the attorney-in-fact as set forth above shall be provided with a copy of my/our attending physician's statement(s), if applicable.

In the event that an activating event occurs and a power of attorney is activated pursuant to this statement, I declare that it is my intention to retain full parental rights to the extent consistent with my condition and circumstances and, further, that I retain the authority to revoke the power of attorney consistent with my rights herein at any time.

This power of attorney shall not be affected by subsequent disability or incapacity of the principal, or also by lapse of time.

SIGNATURE(S) WITH WITNESSES

Parent's Signature:_____ **Date:**_____

Signature of other parent or of parent who shares legal custody with a custodian who signed above:

Parent's Signature:_____ **Date:**_____

Witness's Signature:_____ **Date:**_____
Witness Address:_____

Witness's Signature:_____ **Date:**_____
Witness Address:_____

OPTIONAL NOTARY

STATE OF NEW JERSEY   :
                            : ss.
COUNTY OF _____ :

BE IT REMEMBERED, that on _____, 20___, before me, the subscriber, a Notary Public of the State of New Jersey, personally appeared _____, who, I am satisfied, is the person named in and who executed the foregoing Durable Power of Attorney, and he/she did acknowledge that he/she executed it as his/her voluntary act for the uses and purposes expressed therein.

                                                            _____
                                                            Notary Public

STATE OF NEW JERSEY   :
                            : ss.
COUNTY OF _____ :

BE IT REMEMBERED, that on _____, 20___, before me, the subscriber, a Notary Public of the State of New Jersey, personally appeared _____, who, I am satisfied, is the person named in and who executed the foregoing Durable Power of Attorney, and he/she did acknowledge that he/she executed it as his/her voluntary act for the uses and purposes expressed therein.

                                                            _____
                                                            Notary Public

CHAPTER 17
FORM 11: APPOINTMENT OF AGENT TO CONTROL THE FUNERAL AND DISPOSITION OF REMAINS

LETS INSTRUCTIONS BE GIVEN AND PERSON BE NAMED FOR FUNERAL

This form lets a person give instructions about their funeral and related matters and, also, name a person to manage these things after their death. This book's form is the official form available on the New Jersey Attorney General website.

IN FORM A PERSON CAN BE NAMED AS AGENT TO CONTROL FUNERAL

In the form a person can be named as "Agent" to control funeral and also all related issues after a person's death. <u>If this form isn't done then by law control of all this is by closest family members</u> (in order this means a spouse, children, parents, and siblings). <u>This form is rarely used</u>, mostly only if it seems closest family would do a bad job due to being too upset, being bad with money, or likely to do unwanted things.

IN FORM CAN GIVE INSTRUCTIONS FOR FUNERAL AND DEAD BODY

In the form a person can write instructions about their funeral and similar matters which family, Agent, and others usually must follow if the person's estate can afford it. Detailed instructions can pick the funeral home, church, ceremonies, personnel, invitees, cemetery, tombstone, readings, music, decorations, and food. People can write humble instructions, like "Do cheap Direct Cremation (with no delay or ceremony), wife gets my ashes in urn, in a month do a casual dinner". Some people demand more, like "I want Catholic vigil, funeral mass, and burial service, and use Ox Mortuary". Payment for burial, cremation, ceremonies, and similar things comes from pre-paid funeral accounts, insurance, and a dead person's money and property, and the family and a person's Executor are required to help arrange payment.

PERSON SIGNS AND DATES THE FORM WITH 2 WITNESSES AND NOTARY

For the form to be valid it must be signed and dated a person in the presence of 2 witnesses who then sign too, and a person who is a notary must see the person and witnesses sign and then notarize the form. The form when done should be kept so it can be found within a couple days of a death. To cancel the form a person can tear it up, trash it, mark it cancelled, or clearly tell family it is canceled.

New Jersey Office of the Attorney General
Division of Consumer Affairs
New Jersey Cemetery Board
124 Halsey Street, 6th Floor, P.O. Box 45036
Newark, New Jersey 07101
(973) 504-6553

Appointment of Agent to Control the Funeral and Disposition of Remains

In accordance with N.J.S.A. 45:27-22

General Directions For This Form

- This form creates a Funeral and Disposition Agent ("Agent") who you appoint to authorize your funeral arrangements and the final disposition of your remains after your death. The appointed Agent will have **sole authority** to make decisions regarding your funeral and the final disposition of your remains.

- If you have executed a Last Will and Testament in which a person to control your funeral and disposition is already named, execution of this form will revoke that appointment in favor of the appointment made here. You may appoint as your Agent the same person named as Executor in your Will.

- This form must be signed by you in the presence of two (2) witnesses and a Notary. Both witnesses must sign the completed form, and the Notary must notarize it where indicated.

- You may **NOT** appoint as your Agent any owner, employee, or representative of the funeral home, cemetery or crematory you have chosen/will choose to provide any goods or services related to your funeral and/or the disposition of your remains, unless said person is your relative.

- You may name a successor agent on this form. If your designated Agent(s) is unable or unwilling to act, and no successor agent is named (or the named successor is unable/unwilling to act), the right to control the funeral and disposition of your remains is determined by N.J.S.A. 45:27-22(a). The statute lists the order of priority for the right to control as surviving spouse, then adult children, then parents, then siblings and other next of kin.

Copies of this executed form should immediately be given to the named Agent and any other person who should be informed of the appointment of the Agent, such as the successor agents (if any), funeral home, cemetery or crematory, family members, estate attorney, etc.

New Jersey Office of the Attorney General
Division of Consumer Affairs
New Jersey Cemetery Board
124 Halsey Street, 6th Floor, P.O. Box 45036
Newark, New Jersey 07101
(973) 504-6553

Appointment of Agent to Control the Funeral and Disposition of Remains

I, _____,
(Your name, mailing address, telephone number, email address)

being an adult of sound mind, hereby willfully and voluntarily appoint _____
(Name of Designated Funeral and Disposition Agent)

to serve as my Funeral and Disposition Agent ("Agent"), who, upon my death, shall have authority and power to control and carry out the arrangements for my funeral and the disposition of my remains.

Prior Arrangements:

I ☐ have ☐ have not entered into a pre-need agreement for funeral services and/or merchandise pursuant to N.J.S.A. 45:7-82 et seq.

I ☐ do ☐ do not own an interment space within the cemetery below. Title to the interment space is currently located at: _____

_____

_____

(Name and address of funeral home with which you entered into a pre-need funeral arrangement to provide merchandise and/or services)

(Name and address of cemetery where you own an interment space)

Preferences:

Set forth below are my preferences regarding funeral arrangements and the disposition of my remains. My Agent is not bound by the preferences stated below and may ultimately authorize arrangements and/or final disposition that conflict with any preference listed:

Preferred Funeral Arrangements	Preferred Disposition of Remains

Designated Funeral and Disposition Agent:

Name: _____
Address: _____
Telephone Number: _____
(include area code)

Email Address: _____

Successor Agent Optional:

Name: _____
Address: _____
Telephone Number: _____
(include area code)

Email Address: _____

☐ I choose **not** to name a Successor Agent. I understand that if my designated Agent is unable or unwilling to act, the right to control the funeral and disposition of my remains shall be governed by N.J.S.A. 45:27-22.

This form has been approved by the New Jersey Cemetery Board in accordance with N.J.S.A. 45:27-22.

Authorization:

This appointment becomes effective upon the completion and proper execution of this entire document (witnessed and notarized). At such time, and in so doing, any previous appointment of a person to control the funeral and disposition of my remains is hereby revoked.

In executing this form appointing a Funeral and Disposition Agent, I warrant that all representations and statements contained in this document are true and correct and that all of the statements and signatures are made in order to appoint a Funeral and Disposition Agent. I understand that this appointment supersedes all other priority classes outlined in N.J.S.A. 45:27-22.

Signature of person appointing the Funeral and
Disposition Agent:
_____
Signed this _____ day of _____, 20 _____

Witnesses:

I declare that the person who executed this document above is personally known to me and appears to be of sound mind and acting of his/her free will. He/She signed this document in my presence.

Witness #1:

Name:_____

Address: _____

City:_____ State_____ Zip _____

Signature:_____

Signed this _____ day of _____, 20_____

Witness #2:

Name:_____

Address: _____

City:_____ State_____ Zip _____

Signature:_____

Signed this _____ day of _____, 20_____

Acknowledgement by Notary:

State of New Jersey, County of _____

I certify that the persons named above personally appeared before me, were confirmed and acknowledged to my satisfaction to be the persons identified in this Appointment of Agent to Control the Funeral and Disposition of Remains, and personally signed this document in my presence.

Signed and sworn to before me on this _____ day of _____ , _____

Notary Signature: _____

Notary Name: _____

Expiration of Notary Commission: _____

Affix Seal Here

APPENDIX :
SAMPLE FILLED OUT LEGAL FORMS

TO GET FORMS TO USE PEOPLE CAN:
    (1) PHOTOCOPY BOOK PAGES,
    (2) TEAR OUT PAGES FROM A BOOK, OR
    (3) DOWNLOAD BOOK WITH FORMS FROM WWW.DAVENPORTPUBLISHING.COM
    AND <u>USUALLY PDF FORM AT IS BEST</u> TO AVOID SPACING/FORMAT CHANGES.

EMAIL ANY COMMENTS TO DAVENPORTPRESS@GMAIL.COM.

On the next pages to show how it can be done are some sample filled out legal forms.

People can add words to legal forms by computer or typewriter to be neater, but many people just by hand use pen, marker, or pencil to handwrite words into forms.

It is not required but better if signatures and dates are in ink or marker (not pencil).

Many parts of the forms especially Will gifts can be left empty and unfilled.

Anyone can fill in words in legal form not just the person doing the form, like a friend with neat writing can fill in all the words, addresses, and dates that are needed.
<u>Only the final signatures must be done by each person who wants the</u> form.

To add words in form by pen, pencil, typewriter, or computer any of these is fine:
        "I appoint ___*John Doe*___ as Agent",
        "I appoint ___John Doe___ as Agent",
        "I appoint John Doe as Agent".

When doing forms it may help to know "respectively" means "in order just stated".

People need not worry about neatness or small mistakes, and a document is usually fine if those people who knew a decedent in life can tell the likely meaning.

**Sample Filled Out Form: Last Will and Testament (Standard)
with Gifts section skipped to not bother making small gifts**

LAST WILL AND TESTAMENT

I, __Paul Samuel Maxwell__ , of __Essex County__ , New Jersey do revoke all prior Wills and testamentary documents and do make, publish, and declare this as my Will. I am of sound mind and under no duress or undue influence and acting voluntarily.

1. LIST OF SPOUSE AND CHILDREN. To help show I am mentally competent and have sufficient memory to make a Will I wish to list any living spouse and living children I now have. I currently have the following living spouse and living children:

_____*none*_____

_____.

2. GIFTS. I give these gifts in this Will, but to get a gift in this section the recipient must survive me except as otherwise stated below.

I give _____ to _____.
I give _____ to _____.
I give _____ to _____.
I give _____ to _____.
I give _____ to _____.
I give _____ to _____.

SKIPPED

3. SEPARATE WRITINGS. I may do writings separate from this Will to gift tangible personal property as allowed by state law, and all such writings should be followed. But any such writing not found within 90 days of my death is canceled and has no effect. A gift in such a writing to a person who does not survive me is canceled and has no effect. This Will does not revoke any such writings that now exist.

4. RESIDUE. I give the rest and residue and remainder of my estate, my money and property of any kind and nature, and anything I have an interest in so long as it was not transferred by other Will provisions (all of which is called the "residue"), as follows:

a) to __Susan Lee Maxwell my sister__ who survive me with persons just named who survive me taking the share of non-survivors, then if anything remains

b) to __Oscar David Maxwell and Jennifer Judy Tabor__ and if any of those just named do not survive me their part goes to their lineal descendants, per stirpes.

5. ADMINISTRATION. I nominate and appoint _Susan Lee Maxwell_
as Personal Representative including for me, my Will, and my estate.

6. MISCELLANEOUS. The following applies to this Will and generally.

In this Will no part left unfilled is a mistake including spaces in the residue clause.

The facts support and I want New Jersey state law to apply to this Will and my estate.

I order that my just debts, funeral and related expenses, and taxes be paid as soon after my death as practical but only those items my Personal Representative chooses to pay.

Priority of Will gifts of the same type is based on the order they are written.

The words "give" and "gift" also means a devise, bequest, grant, legacy, or similar.

I am intentionally not providing by Will or other ways for some family, including I am not providing for some children of mine and also children of a deceased child of mine.

If a gift Will reasonably mentions survival then survival is an absolute condition and anti-lapse laws or similar provisions have no effect and without survival the gift lapses. Unless a Will gift specifies otherwise if a Will gift goes to multiple recipients if any do not survive me the part to them lapses and instead goes to other surviving recipients.

No earlier transfer reduces a Will gift unless I usually called it a loan or advancement.

In this Will any gender or gendered word includes all genders, and the singular includes the plural and vice versa, and "they" can mean a single person or many persons.

Unless a Will specifically says otherwise a secured debt including a mortgage or lien shall not be paid off including by a Personal Representative or in probate, and a recipient of a Will gift of property takes it subject to debts. Also, no recipient of property who may lose it or who pays to keep it may have my estate or others pay or do exoneration.

If during my life I disposed of an item in a specific gift then the gift is extinguished.

I request and authorize any informal, summary, and quick probate or similar action. Any Personal Representative may act independently with no supervision of any court, including independent administration, and with no inventory, appraisal, or other action.

I give any Personal Representative the a) fullest authority, discretion, and powers allowed by state law, b) power to lease, sell, mortgage, convey, or keep property including real property in a manner and time they deem helpful or proper, and c) authority to settle or pay claims or debts in the time and manner they choose. Any Personal Representative or other fiduciary shall have all powers and authorities conferred by statute or common law in any jurisdiction they may act, including powers and authorities conferred by Chapter 3B of the New Jersey Statutes Annotated including future amendments.

Any Guardian of any type, Conservator, Custodian, or other person managing a minor's property or money may use or invade the principal and sell property without court action.

If context permits the terms Personal Representative and Executor and Administrator are interchangeable, Conservator and Guardian of the Estate and Guardian of Property and Custodian are interchangeable, and residue and residuary are interchangeable. Any such person may stand in the place of and have all powers like the others named here.

The residue includes lapsed or failed gifts, insurance paid to the estate, digital assets, inheritances owed me, and all I had power of appointment or testamentary disposition over.

Any Personal Representative may access, manage, delete, modify, transfer, and otherwise control any digital accounts and assets I had any interest in or power over.

Any Personal Representative, Executor, Administrator, Guardian of any type like for a person or estate, Conservator, Custodian, and any other fiduciary under this Will or otherwise shall qualify and serve without bond, surety, security, surety bond, or similar.

If evidence does not show it likely a person survived me by 120 hours (5 days) then for this Will and my estate they shall be deemed in all ways as having died before me.

If part of this Will is by law invalid or unenforceable other provisions remain in effect.

Any Personal Representative may at any time transfer money or property of a minor under age 18 to a Custodian to serve under the New Jersey Uniform Transfers to Minors Act or similar law anywhere, and may pick a person to be Custodian including themselves.

TESTATOR

IN WITNESS WHEREOF, I declare that this instrument is my Will which I make as Testator and I have voluntarily signed on the _8th_ day of _June_, 20_22_.

Paul Samuel Maxwell
Testator signature

WITNESSES

The foregoing instrument was signed by the Testator in our presence and declared by the Testator to be the Testator's Will, and we, the undersigned Witnesses, sign our names hereunto acting to witness the Will at the request and in the presence of the Testator, and in the presence of each other on the _8th_ day of _June_, 20_22_.

Susan Ann Moon
Witness #1 signature

14 2nd St., Trenton, NJ 07036
Witness #1 address

Eve Mable Walker
Witness #2 signature

35 Buffalo Road, Denver, Colorado 80101
Witness #2 address

Sample Filled Out Form: Last Will and Testament (Guardian)
with many gifts in Gifts section, Guardian Clause used, and Residue Given By Percentages

LAST WILL AND TESTAMENT

I, __Paul Brian Baker__, of __Freehold Township, New Jersey__, do revoke all prior Wills and testamentary documents and do make, publish, and declare this as my Will. I am of sound mind and under no duress or undue influence and acting voluntarily.

1. LIST OF SPOUSE AND CHILDREN. To help show I am mentally competent and have sufficient memory to make a Will I wish to list any living spouse and living children I now have. I currently have the following living spouse and living children:

_____Ruth May Baker wife_____ _____Oscar Elliot Baker young son_____
_____Karen Lisa Lundy daughter_____ _____Derek Rupert Baker son_____.

2. GIFTS. I give these gifts in this Will, but to get a gift in this section the recipient must survive me except as otherwise stated below.

I give __big oak table__ to __Anne J. Smith__.

I give __$5,000 and Ford Truck__ to __Loretta Marsha Baxter__.

I give __buildings, land, and fixtures at 63 Wentworth Road, Newark, New Jersey,__ to __Kenneth Alan Ford__.

I give __all real property and fixtures I own in Ocean County in New Jersey__ to __Amy Marie Fox and Pamela Sue Fox__.

I give __903 Iceberg Road, Anchorage, Alaska__ to __James Eric Hanson__.

I give __Irish jewelry and my wedding ring__ to __Mary Natalie Swanson__.

I give __all jewelry not given above__ to __Kay Baxter and Mary Baxter__.

I give __$781.35__ to __Mary Natalie Swanson and Kevin Kilby__.

I give __Wells Fargo acct ending in #8923__ to __Lawrence Deer a hunting buddy__.

I give __all spare tires and auto parts__ to __Victor Perez my mechanic__.

I give _____ to _____.

3. SEPARATE WRITINGS. I may do writings separate from this Will to gift tangible personal property as allowed by state law, and all such writings should be followed. But any such writing not found within 90 days of my death is canceled and has no effect. A gift in such a writing to a person who does not survive me is canceled and has no effect. This Will does not revoke any such writings that now exist.

4. RESIDUE. I give the rest and residue and remainder of my estate, my money and property of any kind and nature, and anything I have an interest in so long as it was not transferred by other Will provisions (all of which is called the "residue"), as follows:

  a) to _____Ruth May Baker_____ who survive me with persons just named who survive me taking the share of non-survivors, then if anything remains

  b) to __45% to Oscar Elliot Baker, and 45% to Karen Lisa Lundy, and 10% to Luis Sanchez my friend_____ and if any of those just named do not survive me their part goes to their lineal descendants, per stirpes.

5. ADMINISTRATION. I nominate and appoint __Ruth May Baker_____ as Personal Representative including for me, my Will, and my estate.

6. GUARDIAN. I name, nominate, and appoint _Amanda Sue Brubaker my sister_____ to be Guardian of the Person of any minor child of mine and to have care, authority, custody, and other control of them. I also name this same person to be Guardian of the Estate and Property for any minor child of mine and to have care, control, and power over their property, money, and estate.

7. MISCELLANEOUS. The following applies to this Will and generally.

  In this Will no part left unfilled is a mistake including spaces in the residue clause.

  The facts support and I want New Jersey state law to apply to this Will and my estate.

  I order that my just debts, funeral and related expenses, and taxes be paid as soon after my death as practical but only those items my Personal Representative chooses to pay.

  Priority of Will gifts of the same type is based on the order they are written.

  The words "give" and "gift" also means a devise, bequest, grant, legacy, or similar.

  I am intentionally not providing by Will or other ways for some family, including I am not providing for some children of mine and also children of a deceased child of mine.

  If a gift Will reasonably mentions survival then survival is an absolute condition and anti-lapse laws or similar provisions have no effect and without survival the gift lapses. Unless a Will gift specifies otherwise if a Will gift goes to multiple recipients if any do not survive me the part to them lapses and instead goes to other surviving recipients.

  No earlier transfer reduces a Will gift unless I usually called it a loan or advancement.

  In this Will any gender or gendered word includes all genders, and the singular includes the plural and vice versa, and "they" can mean a single person or many persons.

  Unless a Will specifically says otherwise a secured debt including a mortgage or lien shall not be paid off including by a Personal Representative or in probate, and a recipient of a Will gift of property takes it subject to debts. Also, no recipient of property who may lose it or who pays to keep it may have my estate or others pay or do exoneration.

  If during my life I disposed of an item in a specific gift then the gift is extinguished.

  I request and authorize any informal, summary, and quick probate or similar action.

Any Personal Representative may act independently with no supervision of any court, including independent administration, and with no inventory, appraisal, or other action.

Any Guardian of any type, Conservator, Custodian, or other person managing a minor's property or money may use or invade the principal and sell property without court action.

If context permits the terms Personal Representative and Executor and Administrator are interchangeable, Conservator and Guardian of the Estate and Guardian of Property and Custodian are interchangeable, and residue and residuary are interchangeable. Any such person may stand in the place of and have all powers like the others named here.

The residue includes lapsed or failed gifts, insurance paid to the estate, digital assets, inheritances owed me, and all I had power of appointment or testamentary disposition over.

Any Personal Representative may access, manage, delete, modify, transfer, and otherwise control any digital accounts and assets I had any interest in or power over.

Any Personal Representative, Executor, Administrator, Guardian of any type like for a person or estate, Conservator, Custodian, and any other fiduciary under this Will or otherwise shall qualify and serve without bond, surety, security, surety bond, or similar.

If evidence does not show it likely a person survived me by 120 hours (5 days) then for this Will and my estate they shall be deemed in all ways as having died before me.

If part of this Will is by law invalid or unenforceable other provisions remain in effect.

Any Personal Representative may at any time transfer money or property of a minor under age 18 to a Custodian to serve under the New Jersey Uniform Transfers to Minors Act or similar law anywhere, and may pick a Custodian including themselves.

TESTATOR

IN WITNESS WHEREOF, I declare that this instrument is my Will which I make as Testator and I have voluntarily signed on the __30th__ day of __December__, 20 __21__.

Paul Brian Baker
Testator signature

WITNESSES

The foregoing instrument was signed by the Testator in our presence and declared by the Testator to be the Testator's Will, and we, the undersigned Witnesses, sign our names hereunto acting to witness the Will at the request and in the presence of the Testator, and in the presence of each other on the __30th__ day of __December__, 20 __21__.

Olivia Anna Paulson　　　82 Forest Road, Lakewood, NJ 07134
Witness #1 signature　　　　　Witness #1 address

Matthew John Paulson　　　82 Forest Road, Lakewood, NJ 07134
Witness #2 signature　　　　　Witness #2 address

**Sample Filled Out Form: Last Will and Testament (Standard)
with Will modified to have a 1 Part Residue Clause**

LAST WILL AND TESTAMENT

I, __John David Smith__, of __Bergen County__, New Jersey, do revoke all prior Wills and testamentary documents and do make, publish, and declare this as my Will. I am of sound mind and under no duress or undue influence and acting voluntarily.

1. LIST OF SPOUSE AND CHILDREN. To help show I am mentally competent and have sufficient memory to make a Will I wish to list any living spouse and living children I now have. I currently have the following living spouse and living children:

__my son Adam Michael Smith__
_____.

2. GIFTS. I give these gifts in this Will, but to get a gift in this section the recipient must survive me except as otherwise stated below.

I give __$200__ to __each of my nieces and nephews so about $2,800 in total__.

I give __$400__ to __Garner Food Shelf in Atlantic City, New Jersey__.

I give __$340__ to __my old church Salem Christian Church in Pueblo, Colorado__.

I give _____ to _____.

I give _____ to _____.

I give _____ to _____.

I give _____ to _____.

I give _____ to _____.

I give _____ to _____.

I give _____ to _____.

3. SEPARATE WRITINGS. I may do writings separate from this Will to gift tangible personal property as allowed by state law, and all such writings should be followed. But any such writing not found within 90 days of my death is canceled and has no effect. A gift in such a writing to a person who does not survive me is canceled and has no effect. This Will does not revoke any such writings that now exist.

4. RESIDUE. The rest and residue and remainder of my estate, my property of any kind and nature, and anything I have an interest in, I give to ___Adam Michael Smith and Judy Paula Ford___ who survive me and to the lineal descendants per stirpes of a person just named who did not survive me.

5. ADMINISTRATION. I nominate and appoint ___Judy Paula Ford my sister___ as Personal Representative including for me, my Will, and my estate.

6. MISCELLANEOUS. The following applies to this Will and generally.

In this Will no part left unfilled is a mistake including spaces in the residue clause.

The facts support and I want New Jersey state law to apply to this Will and my estate.

I order that my just debts, funeral and related expenses, and taxes be paid as soon after my death as practical but only those items my Personal Representative chooses to pay.

Priority of Will gifts of the same type is based on the order they are written.

The words "give" and "gift" also means a devise, bequest, grant, legacy, or similar.

I am intentionally not providing by Will or other ways for some family, including I am not providing for some children of mine and also children of a deceased child of mine.

If a gift Will reasonably mentions survival then survival is an absolute condition and anti-lapse laws or similar provisions have no effect and without survival the gift lapses. Unless a Will gift specifies otherwise if a Will gift goes to multiple recipients if any do not survive me the part to them lapses and instead goes to other surviving recipients.

No earlier transfer reduces a Will gift unless I usually called it a loan or advancement.

In this Will any gender or gendered word includes all genders, and the singular includes the plural and vice versa, and "they" can mean a single person or many persons.

Unless a Will specifically says otherwise a secured debt including a mortgage or lien shall not be paid off including by a Personal Representative or in probate, and a recipient of a Will gift of property takes it subject to debts. Also, no recipient of property who may lose it or who pays to keep it may have my estate or others pay or do exoneration.

If during my life I disposed of an item in a specific gift then the gift is extinguished.

I request and authorize any informal, summary, and quick probate or similar action. Any Personal Representative may act independently with no supervision of any court, including independent administration, and with no inventory, appraisal, or other action.

I give any Personal Representative the a) fullest authority, discretion, and powers allowed by state law, b) power to lease, sell, mortgage, convey, or keep property including real property in a manner and time they deem helpful or proper, and c) authority to settle or pay claims or debts in the time and manner they choose. Any Personal Representative or other fiduciary shall have all powers and authorities conferred by statute or common law in any jurisdiction they may act, including powers and authorities conferred by Chapter 3B of the New Jersey Statutes Annotated including future amendments.

Any Guardian of any type, Conservator, Custodian, or other person managing a minor's property or money may use or invade the principal and sell property without court action.

If context permits the terms Personal Representative and Executor and Administrator are interchangeable, Conservator and Guardian of the Estate and Guardian of Property and Custodian are interchangeable, and residue and residuary are interchangeable. Any such person may stand in the place of and have all powers like the others named here.

The residue includes lapsed or failed gifts, insurance paid to the estate, digital assets, inheritances owed me, and all I had power of appointment or testamentary disposition over.

Any Personal Representative may access, manage, delete, modify, transfer, and otherwise control any digital accounts and assets I had any interest in or power over.

Any Personal Representative, Executor, Administrator, Guardian of any type like for a person or estate, Conservator, Custodian, and any other fiduciary under this Will or otherwise shall qualify and serve without bond, surety, security, surety bond, or similar.

If evidence does not show it likely a person survived me by 120 hours (5 days) then for this Will and my estate they shall be deemed in all ways as having died before me.

If part of this Will is by law invalid or unenforceable other provisions remain in effect.

Any Personal Representative may at any time transfer money or property of a minor under age 18 to a Custodian to serve under the New Jersey Uniform Transfers to Minors Act or similar law anywhere, and may pick a person to be Custodian including themselves.

TESTATOR

IN WITNESS WHEREOF, I declare that this instrument is my Will which I make as Testator and I have voluntarily signed on the _21st_ day of ___June___, 20_23_.

John David Smith
Testator Signature

WITNESSES

The foregoing instrument was signed by the Testator in our presence and declared by the Testator to be the Testator's Will, and we, the undersigned Witnesses, sign our names hereunto acting to witness the Will at the request and in the presence of the Testator, and in the presence of each other on the _21st_ day of ___June___, 20_23_.

Mark Elliot Potter   2 Spruce St, Sherwood, N.J. 07411
Witness #1 signature   Witness #1 address

Ann Paula Blom   80 Oak Road, Edison, New Jersey 07124
Witness #2 signature   Witness #2 address

Sample Filled Out Form: Self-Proving Affidavit

SELF-PROVING AFFIDAVIT

(New Jersey Revised Statutes § 3B:3-5)

THE STATE OF NEW JERSEY

COUNTY OF __BERGEN__

We, __John David Smith__, __Mark Elliot Potter__, and __Ann Paula Blom__ the Testator and the Witnesses, respectively, whose names are signed to the attached or foregoing instrument, being duly sworn, do hereby declare to the undersigned authority that the Testator signed and executed the instrument as the Will of Testator and that the Testator had signed willingly, and that the Testator executed it as the Testator's free and voluntary act for the purposes therein expressed, and that each of the Witnesses, in the presence and hearing of the Testator, signed the Will acting to witness the Will and that to the best of the knowledge of each Witness the Testator was at that time 18 years of age or older, of sound mind and under no constraint or undue influence.

_____*John David Smith*_____
Testator

_*Mark Elliot Potter*_____   _____*Ann Paula Blom*_____
Witness   Witness

Subscribed, sworn to, and acknowledged before me by __John David Smith__, the Testator, and subscribed and sworn to before me by __Mark Elliot Potter__ and __Anna Paula Blom__, Witnesses, this __21st__ day of __June__, 20__23__.

(SIGNED) *William P. Jefferson*

(Official capacity of officer) _____

Sample Filled Out Form: Tangible Personal Property List

TANGIBLE PERSONAL PROPERTY LIST

In this writing are gifts of tangible personal property to occur at my death, but this writing if not found by someone within 90 days of my death is canceled.

I may do many pages of these writings which should all be seen as one document. If there are conflicts among such writings the provisions of the more recent writing will revoke the inconsistent provisions of a prior writing.

If a person getting a gift below does not survive me such gift is void and canceled.

DESCRIPTION OF PROPERTY		NAME OF PERSONS TO GET PROPERTY
1998 Ford Truck	to	Samantha Bell
1.3 carat diamond ring + Irish rings	to	Ann Sue Reed
14 ft power boat + kayak + paddles	to	L. Wheeler
Amish style bench	to	Reba Stewart
glass table, telescope, umbrellas	to	Rebecca Stewart
Irish wood cups, oak platter, red vase	to	Mary and Cindy Lott
painting of sailboat in storm	to	Mary Lott
chainsaw with number 382937	to	Mary Lott
chainsaw with number 89930	to	Matt Smith
antique lanterns + repair kits	to	Sue Wu maid at Hart Hotel
lamp kept on porch	to	Mary Kay Poppler
sewing machines	to	Mary Kay Poppler
rocking chair bought in Oregon	to	Don Winkler boat mechanic
all fishing poles and fishing nets	to	Joe "Fish" Hoss, fishing pal
hats at cabin	to	Ken Baker
all clothing except hats at cabin	to	Melissa and Wendy Smith
	to	
	to	
	to	

DATE: 5-15-2024   SIGNED: *John David Smith*

www.ingramcontent.com/pod-product-compliance
Lightning Source LLC
Chambersburg PA
CBHW060416220526
45465CB00008B/2905